Municipal Management & Finances

A Primer for Municipal Officials and other Lay
Persons to help better understand the Basics of
managing a small community.

1ST EDITION

RICHARD NEAL

authorHOUSE®

AuthorHouse™
1663 Liberty Drive
Bloomington, IN 47403
www.authorhouse.com
Phone: 1-800-839-8640

First published by AuthorHouse   01/09/2012

ISBN: 978-1-4685-2966-1 (sc)
ISBN: 978-1-4685-2965-4 (ebk)

Library of Congress Control Number: 2011962811

Printed in the United States of America

Contents

About the Author

Dick Neal was born and raised in Sanford, ME and graduated from Sanford High School in 1950. After high school, he attended the University of Maine, majoring in Wildlife Conservation. From 1951 to 1955, he served in the U.S. Air Force as a Radio Maintenance Technician. Upon discharge in 1955, he enrolled at the University of New Hampshire in the Electrical Engineering Program. He graduated in 1959 with a BSEE. Upon graduation, he went to work at the Portsmouth Naval Shipyard and retired in 1986 after working 27 years as an Electronics Engineer in the Combat Systems Office. During the last 15 years of his career, he served as a Weapons Systems Manager on Submarines managing some of the world's largest and most complex weapon systems in the world. While working at the Portsmouth Naval Shipyard, he lived in the Town of Sanford with his wife Rhea where they raised five children. During this same period, he was active in municipal affairs such as the Warrant & Finance Committee and the Planning Board. He was also on the Board of Trustees for the Goodall Memorial Library for 5 years and served on several School Building Committees. In 1987, he moved, with his wife, Rhea, to a 200+ year old farmhouse in Acton on the Milton Mills Road next to the school. In 1989, he was elected as Selectman/Assessor, where he completed three 3-year terms. During his tenure as Selectman/Assessor, he became a Certified Maine Assessor in 1993 and has written many of the Town of Acton policies, procedures and ordinances. He has served on many of the town committees and was the E911 Coordinator for the Town of Acton from 1998 to 2005. From 1998 to 2001, he served as EMA Director for the Town of Acton. He has been the Secretary of the Maine Federation of the National Active and Retired Federal Employees Association from 2003 to 2010. In 2010, he was elected 2nd Vice President of the Maine Federation.

In 1996, he was appointed by the Governor to the Inland Fisheries & Wildlife Advisory Council and served two 3-year terms. He has a wealth of experience with over thirty years of working with various fish and game clubs and 65 years as an angler and hunter. He is a past president of the Sanford/ Springvale Fish & Game club and the Associated Sportsmen's Club of York County. He is also on the Board of Directors of the Saco River Salmon Club and the Three Rivers Land Trust. In 2009, he was elected Vice President of the Saco River Salmon Club.

Introduction

Being a Municipal Officer or Municipal Official can be a challenging task in many of the small communities in Maine or any other state. Most of these positions are part time and do not draw the best of salaries. Unfortunately, there is little training and no certification requirements for these positions. In many cases, newly elected officers or elected/appointed officials depend on the past practices of their predecessors. These past practices may be OK or not OK and may not meet today's standards. The budgets are much bigger and there are more state and federal laws/regulations to comply with. In the State of Maine, the Maine Municipal Association (MMA) offers some basic training/workshops and provides legal counsel for member communities for those that choose to participate. Many are not willing to spend the time in attending these training classes/workshops.

I have been intimately involved with Municipal Government for over 47 years. I have served on the Warrant and Finance (Budget) Committee, Appeals Board, Planning Board, Board of Assessment Review, Comprehensive Planning Committee, Capital Improvement Committee and numerous Building Committees. I have also served on the Board of Directors of various civic organizations. I was a Selectman in the Town of Acton for over 9 ½ years and also served as the Town of Acton EMA Director and E911 Coordinator for a number of years. In 1993, I became a Certified Maine Assessor.

This book is really a compilation of many of the papers, policies and procedures that I have written over the years. It is my desire to pass on to others, many of the things that I have learned. Being a selectman or any other municipal official is not an easy task and requires a lot of time and hard work to do the job right. I was always taught that if you are going to do a job, then make sure that you do it right.

I hope that the information that I have presented is informative and helpful to other Municipal Officers, Municipal Officials and to the laymen that might be interested in the many aspects of running a municipal government.

I wish to thank all those who have contributed to helping me with this project and especially to my good friend and neighbor, Jerry Nulton, for his help in formatting. Over the years, I have gained much of my information from the Maine Municipal Association and from a Manual by Robert Reny, entitled "Model Finance and Accounting Procedures". For more detailed information, I recommend contacting the Maine Municipal Association.

If anyone has any comments, questions or corrections, feel free to call me at 207-636-3205 or email me at [ran@metrocast.net].

Richard Neal

Chapter 1

The Selectman's Role

Understanding the Selectman's Job

Historically in Maine, the person elected to a town's board of municipal officers, whether male or female, has been referred to as the town <u>selectman</u>. In fact, the term "selectman" is still found throughout Maine's Statutes, although in recent years the Legislature has been using the term "municipal officers" for "selectman" when enacting new municipal legislation.

There are probably two reasons for the Legislature's current preference for the term "municipal officer". First, the term could reflect a conscious effort to steer Maine law toward gender neutrality. Also, 30-A MRSA 2001 defines a "municipal <u>officer</u>" as the "selectman or councilor of a town, or the mayor and alderman or councilor of a city." In that same section of law, the term "municipal <u>official</u>" is defined as "any elected or appointed member of a municipal government." What distinguishes the municipal officers from all other municipal officials is the broad range of authority and responsibility granted to the municipal officers as the town's <u>chief executive officers</u>. For these reasons, the term "municipal officers" is used throughout this paper in the place of "selectman.

It is difficult to overestimate the depth and range of responsibilities that are associated with a municipal officers duties of office. New England enjoys a unique tradition of significant municipal authority, and Maine's towns and cities have been given a larger share of governmental responsibility than municipalities in many other states. Along with the privilege of this under a town meeting form of government, almost all of the responsibilities fall upon the board of municipal officers either directly or indirectly.

Most people who have never been a municipal officer are completely unaware of the complexities of modern municipal administration. After a person is sworn in as a municipal officer, the range of duties alone can seem formidable: financial administration; solid waste disposal; assessing; welfare; employee supervision and personnel relations; road supervision; the appointments and supervision of a galaxy of municipal officials, boards and committee members; public management; contract administration; intergovernmental coordination; record keeping; legal affairs; communications. These are just a few aspects of the job, and this fails to mention the part of the job that is perhaps the most important and certainly the most time consuming: attention to the grievances, needs, aspirations, and interests of the public which are being served.

Few jobs are as potentially rewarding as is that of the municipal officer, or as potentially frustrating. The look, feel and personality of a community can be changed dramatically, for the good or for the bad, not only by the major decisions made by the board of municipal officers, but also by the administrative practices or the attitudes that the municipal officers might adopt toward the public or other governmental agencies with which they might deal. In order to maintain the trust and respect of others, they must act in the most ethical manner at all times and must hold all other municipal officials, employees and volunteers accountable to the same high ethical standards. Chapter 6 contains a sample Code of Ethics.

Duties and Powers: Executive Functions

Under a town meeting form of government, the duty of the municipal officers is to <u>execute</u> the "Will of the people" as that "Will" that has been expressed legislatively by the Town Meeting Body. In a town meeting town, therefore, the municipal officers and all the other municipal officials either elected or appointed by the municipal officers) represents the <u>executive branch</u> of the municipal government, of which the municipal officers are the chief executive officers.

The specific duties of a town's chief executive officer are many and varied. In an effort to categorize those duties, however, it is helpful to think of the town as a corporation, which is exactly what it is—a municipal corporation. In order to safeguard and advance the interests of a municipal corporation, the chief executive officer, acting as the agent for the legislative body, is ultimately responsible for four broad areas of corporate management:

- Management of the municipal finances
- Protecting the health, safety and welfare of the municipal residents
- Public property and personnel management
- The municipal officers are the representatives of the town for intergovernmental and public relations purposes.

Executive/Administrative Role

The Executive/Administrative duties and responsibilities are wide and varied. The following areas and functions are common to most small to middle sized towns.

Municipal Officers Meetings

Depending on the size of the community, the municipal officers may have their regular meetings scheduled weekly, monthly or bimonthly depending on the amount of business to be conducted. State law does not require that the municipal officers meet with any regularity. Any meeting other than a regular meeting is called a special or emergency meeting. Quorum and notice requirements apply to both types of meetings. Municipal officers have a responsibility to know and follow the laws concerning:

- Notice Requirements
- Public Participation
- Right to Know
- Executive Sessions
- Public Records
- Conduct of Meetings

Town Meeting and Town Meeting Warrant

All legislative action by the voters must be done through the town meeting. All towns must hold an annual town meeting to elect officials 30-A MRSA § 2525. Generally, budget items and other business items are voted on at the annual meeting.

The municipal officers have the authority to set the date of the annual town meeting unless spelled out differently by ordinance or charter. They also set the date for special town meetings.

The municipal officers generally determine the wording and placement of the articles in the town meeting warrant. They are responsible for reviewing each article to make sure that it is unambiguous and does not call for any action that might be illegal or improper. The municipal officers should also make sure that each article is something that the voters have the legal right to vote on.

The municipal officers are responsible for ensuring that the town meeting warrants are properly posted.

Personnel

An important executive duty is dealing with personnel. The municipal officers are responsible for the hiring, firing, discipline, productivity, and supervision of appointed officials and hired employees (those people employed by the town but who do not take an oath of office, such as the solid waste attendants, secretarial staff, and so on). Under a town manager or administrator these duties may be delegated, but it is a good idea for the municipal officers to know the general rules in this area.

Public Property

The municipal officers have a general obligation as executive officers to ensure that public property is not destroyed, wasted or misused. Public property may be "real" property (land and buildings) or "personal" property (vehicles, equipment, cash, and the like). Specific items of property are discussed below. In many cases, a town board or commission may also have some involvement with property.

The Municipal Officers are responsible for the proper maintenance of all public property and taking appropriate action to correct problems that are brought to their attention.

Cemeteries
The state law governing cemeteries is found in 13 MRSA § 1031-1349, and include private as well as public burial grounds. The town has a duty (§1101) to maintain the graves of U.S. veterans who served in any war.

Private cemeteries may be conveyed to the town in accordance with §§ 1221-1222, and the town may administer perpetual care of similar trust accounts in accordance with §§1223-1263.

The ownership, operation and maintenance of public cemeteries are governed by §§1302-1305.

Parks and Playgrounds
Areas designed and maintained for public recreation are generally overseen by an elected or appointed commission or a recreation department. In either case, the municipal officers should know whether insurance is needed for these areas. Also, if private concessions or events are located in a public park, the municipal officers must be involved in the contract process.

Fields and Forests
The town may own land, which is not designed or intended for recreational use. These areas may be open to the public, but the municipal officers should take steps to prevent litter, pollution, tree cutting and other problems, which devalue or destroy the property. Conservation commissions often have a role in this regard, making recommendations on how to preserve these lands. The town municipal officers may want to draft an ordinance (for town approval) restricting the use of these lands.

Ministerial and School Lands
Many towns hold title to what is known as "ministerial and school land". The state law governing this is found at 13 MRSA §§3161-3172. The municipal officers, town clerk and treasurer serve as trustees of these lands if no other trustees exist.

Libraries
The law governing public libraries is found at 27 MRSA §101-109. The municipal officers are responsible for the operation of any town-owned library and may appoint one or more persons to actually run the library on a day-to-day basis. In many towns, the town may own the building, but the "public" library is operated by a Board of Trustees. If that is the case, the municipal officers do not have decision-making authority over the trustees or over property owned by the library corporation. Commonly, the library is financially supported by the town and by a private endowment. It may require some research to determine the town's obligations and powers if this is the case.

Tax-acquired Property
The town often takes title to property because the owner failed to pay property taxes or certain other assessments in the time allowed. With town approval, the municipal officers may sell this property to recover the taxes and get the property back on the tax rolls. The town may want to keep the property

for a park or other purposes, in which case the municipal officers should oversee it as explained above. Where the taxpayer continues to reside on the property after the tax lien forecloses, the town may still authorize the sale of the property, but the municipal officers should make it clear to any purchaser that eviction is the purchaser's responsibility. The property should be sold by quitclaim deed (not warranty deed) and the municipal officers should make no representations about the value or condition of the property or quality of title. In terms of liability, the town is not liable for injuries occurring on the property until 60 days after the former owner or tenant has given up actual possession. At that point, municipal officers should make certain that the property is not a safety hazard and is adequately insured. This may require that the place be boarded up or otherwise sealed. Municipal Officers should, periodically, check the inventory of Tax-Acquired Property to see if there are any that should be disposed of and put back on the tax rolls. Disposal of Town-owned Property must be authorized by the Town Meeting

Town-owned Buildings
A town may own and operate several buildings, such as the town hall, garage, fire station, library and other facilities. The municipal officers must see to it that these building are adequately insured against damage as well as for liability. Also, the municipal officers should keep track of the physical condition of the buildings, grounds and parking areas so that maintenance and repairs can be done before small problems become large ones.

Vehicles and Equipment
Regardless which department uses town vehicles or equipment, the municipal officers should make sure that these items are adequately insured and regularly maintained.

Roads

The municipal officers are responsible for ensuring that the town ways (public roads and streets) are maintained and used properly. The following list indicates areas that the municipal officers may be involved:

    Creating Roads
    Discontinuing roads by formal town meeting vote
    Abandoning roads by passage of time
    Winter closings
    Seasonal, emergency and special event closings
    Weight restrictions
    Controlling vehicles, parking and pedestrians
    Liability
    Snow removal and road maintenance
    Utility pole permits
    Salt/sand sheds
    Contaminated wells

One of the municipal officer's major involvements with roads in some communities is with the property owners that live on unaccepted roads and continually request that the town provide services such as plowing, sanding, grading and repairing of their unaccepted road. The municipal officers must listen to these complaints or requests and try to explain that the town is not allowed by law to expend public funds on any unaccepted ways.

Public Safety

The municipal officers as executive officers are responsible to ensure that the public safety measures that have been implemented in their community are enforced fairly and equitably. This includes police protection, ordinance enforcement, fire and emergency services, animal control, dangerous buildings and nuisances, public health and civil defense.

Solid Waste Management

The municipal officers are responsible for the proper disposal of solid waste generated within their community. In recent years, most Maine communities have come under increased pressure by the State to close their local landfills and to also start recycling programs. The costs for closing the landfills, building transfer stations and establishing recycling programs are staggering. These problems and the headaches that go with them are taking more and more of the municipal officer's time.

General Assistance

The municipal officers are the "Overseers of the Poor" unless and until they have designated another person or persons as the municipal officials charged with that function. The overseers are responsible for administering the towns General assistance program, which is a municipal program mandated by state law (22 MRSA §44301 et seq.). The operation of the town's GA program is discussed in detail in MMA's General Assistance Manual.

Litigation and Ordinance Enforcement

One important executive function of the municipal officers is to decide if and when the town should file a lawsuit in a particular situation. This often arises in the context of an ordinance violation, where a lawsuit may be the only way to obtain compliance. The town may need to bring suit in other matters as well. For example; breach of contract, destruction or misuse of town property or to clear up boundary or road disputes. The municipal officers are the only town officials with the authority to bring an action in the town's name. The Planning Board or some other official may want to sue but they must do it through the municipal officers. The municipal officers make the decision whether to got to court or not but the money needed to do this must be authorized by the voters.

Duties and Powers: Legislative and Quasi-Judicial Functions

Legislative Role

While the municipal officers have very broad executive powers, their legislative or law making powers are limited to what is granted by state law, local charter or ordinance. The municipal officers can adopt a personnel policy that describes the rights and duties of town employees or a policy on how to run their meetings. A policy cannot be used to regulate outside matters such as automobile junkyards, parking, victualers, etc. Those matters must be controlled by ordinance or regulation. Although the municipal officers are limited in their ability to enact ordinances in general, they are responsible to prepare or have someone else prepare any ordinance deemed necessary to resolve a local problem and submit it to a town meeting for action.

Despite the fact that the town meeting is the town's legislative body, Maine law describes a few legislative functions that are to be performed by the municipal officers. The following list comprises some of these functions:

- Cable TV ordinances pursuant to 30-A MRSA §3008 and 3010
- All traffic ordinances pursuant to 30-A MRSA §3009
- General Assistance ordinances pursuant to 22 MRSA §4305
- Regulation of lands over or adjacent to public water supplies pursuant to 22 MRSA §2642
- An ethics policy governing the conduct of elected and appointed officials pursuant to 30-A MRSA §2605(7)
- Regulations on the temporary or seasonal use of roads pursuant to 29 MRSA §902
- Extension of a moratorium ordinance, which was already adopted by the town pursuant to 30-A MRSA §4356

Quasi-Judicial Role

When the municipal officers are called upon formally to hear facts and to make a decision, they are performing a quasi-judicial function since this is what a judge does in court. This duty most commonly arises in issuing permits and licenses. 30-A MRSA §3701 states that the municipal officers are the town's licensing authority unless otherwise provided by statue, charter or ordinance.

In the conduct of personnel matters, the municipal officers are often responsible for the hiring, supervision and firing of employees or appointed officials. State law and court cases set some guidelines in this regard and the town may have a personnel policy, union contract or charter provision which describes how to conduct personnel matters. Before taking any disciplinary action, the municipal officers must investigate the complaint—this is essentially a fact-finding duty. The employee involved, has the right to present his/her side of the story. The municipal officers make their decision based on the information presented.

Other Matters

The municipal officers may be asked to make other quasi-judicial decisions such as declaring a building to be dangerous-17MRSA §2851 or deeming a road to be abandoned-23MRSA §3028.

Interaction with other Municipal Officials, Boards and Committees

Assessor

Historically, and in many towns today, the board of municipal officers also serves as the board of assessors. For many boards of municipal officers who undertake the entire assessing function, the assessing chore is by far the most time consuming task associated with being a municipal officer. A relatively recent trend in even the smallest towns is to contract out the appraising component of the assessing function. This is almost always done when it comes time for the town to do a complete revaluation. Many towns continue with the use of a professional appraiser for an annual maintenance service, particularly for new property valuations.

It is important to remember that the professional appraiser employed by the town for the purpose of appraising property values is not the town assessor unless expressly appointed by the board of municipal officers, pursuant to 30-A MRSA §2526. The private appraiser under contract only provides information to the assessors, which they may or may not use in determining the actual assessment. For this reason, it is important for the municipal officers to understand the methods used by the appraiser.

In general, the board of assessors has the following basic responsibilities:

- Maintain an updated mapping system depicting all parcels of land in the community. This requires a review of all deed transfers so that any subdivision of lots may be recorded on the tax maps and that proper square footage or acreage may be recorded.
- Maintain updated lists of all real and personal property so that taxes may be assessed to the proper owner of record.
- Maintain an updated list of all exempt property.
- Perform field inspections to determine pertinent data concerning the land, buildings, structures, equipment and any other improvements. A review of all building and plumbing permits help to identify which properties need to be inspected for revaluation.
- Determine value of property. After collecting general, specific and comparative data on all types of property, the assessor analyzes the data and processes them into indications of value for each individual piece of property. The property is then assessed at its market value or at some legally authorized fraction thereof, known as the assessed value.
- Determine the classification of all land and properties into their proper category. This includes "tree growth", "farmland", "open space", "shore land", "resource protection", "general purpose" and various "exemptions".
- Update records and maintaining the official Valuation Book.
- Certify the Valuation Book and determining the tax rate.

- Provide the Tax Collector with the "Tax Commitment Book" consisting of a list of valuations and the individual assessments. It also contains the Collector's Warrant, a certificate of commitment and a certificate to the effect that the list is a "perfect list of assessments.
- Review requests for abatements and taking the necessary action to grant or deny and abatements.
- Represent the community during public hearings before the Board of Assessment Review.
- Make supplemental assessments. At times, certain additional or supplementary assessments may be necessary in cases where persons or property were inadvertently omitted from the regular assessment.

All newly elected Municipal Officers, whether they intend to become a Certified Maine Assessor or not, should attend some of the Assessor's Training Courses, sponsored by Maine Revenue Services to learn the basics of assessing.

Tax Collector

The municipal property tax collector is elected or appointed for the purpose of collecting all property taxes assessed by the assessors against all real estate and personal property.

The principal interaction of the municipal officers and the tax collector is when the municipal officers are also the assessors. The assessors provide the tax collector with the "Tax Commitment Book" which the tax collector uses as a basis for the collection of taxes.

Town Clerk

The town clerk is essentially the keeper of records and documents for the community. The town clerk also performs many important duties in connection with local, state and federal elections. The town clerk acts as an agent of various state departments in the issuance of licenses and permits.

The municipal officers are required to provide a fire proof safe or vault to the town clerk to use for the preservation of all records that are not current records.

Treasurer

The general duties of the treasurer are to receive and record all revenues due the municipality and to make necessary disbursements to retire all municipal debts only upon authorization of the board of municipal officers. Although the treasurer is certainly an important and primary adviser to the municipal officers with regard to financial matters, the treasurer is prohibited from acting in an unauthorized or unilateral way, such as choosing banking or lending institutions, making unauthorized disbursements of any kind, setting financial policy or initiating loans. The treasurer may disburse money only on a warrant for that purpose signed by a majority of the municipal officers.

Road Commissioners

Both the municipal officers, generally, and the road commissioners, specifically, are responsible for ensuring that the town ways and bridges are safe and convenient for travelers with motor vehicles. (23 MRSA §3651). At times there may be some confusion as to the relationship between the road commissioners and the municipal officers because the road commissioners are often elected positions and cannot be removed or formally disciplined by the municipal officers. 23 MRSA §2701 states:

> "In the absence of a statue, charter provision or ordinance to the contrary, any decision involving the duties and responsibilities of the road commissioner shall be made by a majority of the selectmen, whose decision shall be final."

The road commissioners, therefore, while in charge of highway repair and maintenance within the town, must act according to the general policies or guidelines as determined by the municipal officers. Unless the town uses a specific line-item budget, the municipal officers have the authority to decide how money will be spent regarding road work and road personnel. The road commissioner has no inherent authority to incur expenses or enter contracts for the town. This can only be done if authorized by the municipal officers.

The municipal officers, in conjunction with inputs from the road commissioners, are responsible for going out to bid for paving or other contract work in the building or maintenance of the town roads. All bids should contain specifications to ensure that proper work and materials are provided.

Fire Department

There are three different ways to provide fire protection for a town and the control over the department will vary according to the method used for fire protection in your community. A town is not required by law to provide fire protection at all. Most towns do have some sort of fire department or contract out for fire protection, but this is a discretionary service.

Every town must have a fire chief. Strange as it seems, the law (30-A MRSA § 3153) does require a town to have a fire chief even though a town is not required to provide fire protection. The municipal officers establish the compensation of the fire chief.

Many small towns have a volunteer fire department (VFD), which may vary in organization from town to town. Some VFD's are independent and are not a department of the town at all. They elect their own officers, own their own equipment and property. Their financial accounts are kept separate from the town. The municipal officers have no direct control over these fire departments.

In other towns, the land, firehouse, fire trucks and equipment are provided and owned by the town. Operating funds are provided by the town meeting and the municipal officers generally appoint the fire chief unless spelled out otherwise by charter or ordinance. Requests for and disbursement of funds are made through the municipal officers. Fire fighters may be volunteer, full time, part time or on-call.

A third method of fire protection authorized by 30-A MRSA §3152 is for the town to contract out with another town or VFD that may be willing to provide the service. The municipal officers would be responsible for negotiating the contract and submitting it to the town meeting for approval.

School Board

Schools in Maine are governed by elected school boards which have certain duties prescribed by law 20-A MRSA §1001. Two areas where the municipal officers are generally involved in education are:

First, there is a financial link between the municipal officers and the school board, particularly with regard to municipal schools. For the SAD or the CSD, the municipal officers are billed for the town's pro-rata share of educational services in accordance with a budget approved by the voters in the SAD or CSD. The municipal officers authorize the treasurer to pay the bills just as they would handle any other debt.

For the municipal schools (see 20-A MRSA §2301 et seq.), the municipal officers involvement is deeper because the municipal officers must review and approve all school related disbursements on a case by case basis, just as they would for any other town expenditures. As the town's chief executive officers, the Municipal Officers have the authority to question and may refuse to authorize any <u>municipal </u>school disbursement, which was not authorized by the town meeting. In fact, the municipal officers could incur personal financial liability for a school overdraft, just as they could for an overdraft from any other line budget item.

The other area of interaction between the school board (or its administrative staff) and the municipal officers concerns the use of municipal services such as solid waste disposal, fire protection, traffic control, plowing, etc. In return for any special demands for municipal services, school facilities are regularly made available for town functions. In order to coordinate this exchange of services, it is important to maintain good communication between the municipal officers and the school board.

Other Boards and Committees
The board of municipal officers has the responsibility to appoint the members of local boards, committees, and commissions unless otherwise directed by local charter, ordinance or state statue. Specifics of such appointments may be found in the charter or ordinance provisions that created the board or committee in question.

The municipal officers are responsible for knowing what the overall responsibilities of the individual boards and committees are and ensuring that they fulfill those responsibilities and act in accordance with the charter, ordinance or state statue.

Interaction with other Municipalities, the Private Sector and the State

Dealing with other Municipalities

Municipalities often find it desirable or necessary to join with other municipalities to deal with problems such as solid waste, recycling, and police/fire protection or road maintenance. To do this, the municipal officers usually enter an agreement or contract with the municipal officers of the other municipality. Although the voters have to approve the agreement or contract, the municipal officers, on behalf of the municipality, are responsible for seeing that the provisions, contained within, are met.

Dealing with the Private Sector

Most transactions with private businesses are done by contract. The voters need not approve the specific contract itself; they may authorize the municipal officers to enter a contract for so many years or for so many dollars. The board of municipal officers must use its judgment in negotiating the specific contract and attempt to do what is in the best interest of the municipality within the authority granted by the voters. There is no state law that generally requires that town work be put out to bid. Certain projects such as school construction and state mandated public improvements must follow the bid rules contained in 5 MRSA §§and 1743A. Some municipalities have a charter or ordinance which requires that a bid process be used.

Dealing with the States

The areas where the municipal officers interact with the state government are far too numerous to describe in detail. On a day-to-day basis, the municipal officers deal with the various departments within the executive branch of the state government. There is a need also for the municipal officers to communicate with their area legislators.

Financial Matters

Municipal finance is without question one of the most important and time consuming responsibilities facing any board of municipal officers. Because many new municipal officers come into office without any special expertise in financial management, there is sometimes the tendency not to question the town's traditional financial management systems.

Municipal expenditures have increased dramatically in the last 5-10 years for most communities. Therefore it is incumbent on all municipal officers to become informed and knowledgeable of the proper financial procedures. The municipal officers, as the chief executive officers of their community, are responsible for ensuring that all revenues and expenditures are accounted for and that proper records are maintained. They are also responsible to ensure that any use of revenues and disbursement of funds are made only in accordance with the direction of the town meeting articles as voted on.

The task of financial planning and financial administration consists of the following components:

Budgeting
Revenue Source Identification
Bonding, Borrowing and Debt Limits
Investments
Reviewing all Bills and Authorizing Payment
Proper Record Keeping
Proper Accounting Procedures
Annual Audits
Capital Improvement Planning
Cash Flow Analysis

Municipal officers should obtain a rudimentary knowledge of the Municipal Accounting System so that they can understand the Municipal Financial Reports/Audit Reports. More detail is covered in Chapter 2.

Note: Most of the information for this synopsis of what a Selectman's job is all about came from the "Handbook for Municipal Officers", put out by the Maine Municipal Association. I had the pleasure of working with Joe Wathen in the preparation of the Handbook in 1990 and 1991. I had been elected a Selectman, in the Town of Acton, in 1989 and didn't have a clue as to what the job was all about. In my search for information, I called MMA and ended up talking with Joe Wathen. He asked me to participate in the preparation of the Handbook and I agreed. This chapter is just a synopsis of what a Selectman's job is. In May, 2000, the "Handbook for Municipal Officers" was revised and renamed "Municipal Officer's Manual". For more detail, refer to the "Municipal Officers Manual" and the "Assessors Manual". They are both available from MMA. I strongly recommend that any newly elected Municipal Officer take advantage of the Training Sessions/Seminars sponsored by MMA and Maine Revenue Services. I also encourage municipal officers to attend the MMA Convention, generally held in September or October each year. I have found it very informative and well worth the time and cost to attend.

Chapter 2

Municipal Finances

Forward

The purpose of this chapter is to provide Municipal Officers and other Municipal Officials tips and information on the basics of Municipal Accounting and other Municipal Financial Processes. Understanding these basics is essential for the proper management of the financial affairs of any community. These tips and info are directed, mainly, to the Municipal Officers and other Municipal Officials such as members of the Warrant & Finance (Budget) Committee and members of the local School Board.

I was elected to the Board of Selectmen in the Town of Acton in 1989. It was also the year that the town transitioned into the computer age. I soon realized that the town was changing. Our population was increasing, the demand for services was increasing and our budget was growing proportionally. One system in need of change was our financial system. Going to a computerized accounting system was only the first step in the many changes to come.

One of the significant events that prompted me to take action was in 1991, as Chairman of the Board of Selectmen, I couldn't wait for the results of our annual audit for the previous year. As chair, I had been conservative with my Revenue budget and made sure that there were no overdrafts in the Appropriations. When I looked at the "Undesignated Fund Balance", I was shocked to see that it was a negative number. How could that be, I asked the auditor. He could not explain it. His response was, that in accordance with the financial equation used in Municipal Accounting, "Assets—Liabilities = Fund Balance", he could measure our assets and liabilities. By subtracting the liabilities from the assets, he could come up with the Fund Balance. The Fund Balance was made up of a Designated Fund Balance and an Undesignated Fund Balance. The Designated Fund Balance consisted of the Balances carried forward by the Town Meeting Articles. By subtracting the Designated Fund Balance from the overall Fund Balance, the amount left was the Undesignated Fund Balance. This event caused me to spend countless hours in discussions with other Selectmen, Town Managers, Finance Directors, Auditors and others in my quest for more information on Municipal Accounting and other Municipal Finances.

To the best of my knowledge, the information contained in this chapter is not available in any one current document. This chapter is a compilation of information that I have accumulated from various sources over the last 20 years. It includes various policies, rules and procedures developed for the Town of Acton during my nine-and-a-half years as a Selectman. The information in this chapter is, also offered to others who may be interested in understanding and providing better management of the financial affairs of their community.

Introduction to the Basics of Municipal Accounting

This section provides an introduction to the Basics of Municipal Accounting. It should provide you with a basic familiarity to read and understand the various financial reports, necessary for the proper management of the financial affairs of your community.

The Municipal Accounting System consists of:

1. Source Documents—Source Documents are the original documents that provide the necessary detail, such as checks, receipts, invoices, time cards, purchase orders and various forms (request for payment or reimbursement) that have been signed by an authorized official.
2. Journals (Books of Original Entry)—Journals are used to make the first formal recording of a financial transaction. The data is, generally, taken from a source document. The four most common types of journal are, cash receipts journal, cash disbursements journal, payroll journal and a general journal for all entries not recorded in one of the other journals.
3. Ledgers—Ledgers record the summary totals of the transactions from the journals. They provide the balances in any account at a given point in time. The General Ledger (GL) consists of an individual account sheet for every Asset, Liability, Revenue, Expense and Capital Account in use by a given municipality.
4. There may be times when more detailed records are required than is practical in the General Ledger. For those transactions, a Subsidiary Ledger is used. Examples of Subsidiary Ledgers are Revenue Control, Expense (Appropriation) Control, Current Taxes Receivable and Tax Liens.
5. Procedures and Controls—It is recommended that every municipality have a written "Financial Policy and Procedures Manual". The manual, not only establishes the policy to be followed in the municipal financial system, but also provides the forms and standardized procedures necessary to classify, record, summarize, control and report information correctly in the accounting system. It also provides everyone involved with the knowledge of who is responsible for what. The manual may include many of the sections found in this guide.

General Ledger

The General Ledger is the centerpiece of Municipal Accounting. It provides the balances in any one account at a given point in time. It is laid out in the format of the basic accounting equation used in Municipal Accounting.

Assets-Liabilities = Fund Balance

The Assets are listed at the top of the General Ledger, followed by Liabilities and ending with Fund Balance accounts and other Equity Accounts. Municipal Accounting utilizes a double-entry bookkeeping system. The General Ledger is laid out in the form of a "**T**", with Debits on the left side and Credits on the right side. The Assets and Expense Accounts are listed as a Debit (on the left side) and the Liabilities, Fund Balance and Revenue Accounts are listed as a Credit (on the right side). When a transaction is entered into the General Ledger, the entry will include at least one debit and one credit. The Debits must always equal the Credits. For example, if someone was to make a payment on their RE taxes, there would be a Credit (decrease) entry for Taxes Receivable and a Debit (increase) entry in the Cash account. If a Grant were received, there would be a Credit (increase) in the Revenue account and a Debit (increase) in the Cash account. A balance is always maintained in all the accounts with the total of all the Debit entries equaling the total of all the Credit entries. This provides the basic proof of accuracy for the Double-Entry Bookkeeping System.

Fund Accounting

Municipal Accounting is also known as Fund Accounting. Most of the accounts associated with the operation of a Municipality are grouped into what is called the "General Fund". Other funds may be established when revenues and expenditures need to be tracked separately. It is recommended that the number of funds be kept to a minimum.

Cash vs. Accrual Basis of Accounting

In a Cash Basis of Accounting, revenues are recognized when actually received and expenses are recorded when actually paid. In a Full Accrual Basis of Accounting, revenues are recorded at the time they are earned. The expenses are recorded when the liability is incurred. Most municipalities use what is known as the Modified Accrual Basis of Accounting, where the revenues are recorded when they are measurable and available. Expenses are generally recognized and recorded when the liability is incurred as under the Full Accrual Basis. Some small municipalities may still be using the Cash Basis method. The Modified Accrual basis is the preferred method for the municipal accounting systems General Fund. All Nonexpendable Trust Funds, such as Cemetery Trust Funds or School Scholarship Funds utilize the Full Accrual Basis of Accounting.

Reports

In order to properly manage their areas of responsibility, the Municipal Officers and other Municipal Officials need to review and understand various periodical financial reports. Certain interim Financial Reports should be reviewed on a monthly basis. The monthly Revenue and Expenditure reports should have the Budgeted Amount and the Actual Amount listed for each account. Some systems also have a column that shows the percentage of the budgeted amounts received or expended.

It is recommended that the following financial reports be submitted to the Municipal Officers for their review, on a monthly basis:

Expense Report—This report lists the Budgeted Expenditures as appropriated by the Town Meeting and the Actual Amounts Expended.

Revenue Report—This report lists the Estimated Revenues that are to be used to reduce the amount to be raised by taxation and the Actual Amounts Received.

Trial Balance Report of the General Ledger (It is important for the total balance to be equal for the Debit and Credit columns.)

At the end of the year, there should be a final report that shows the total figures for each account that have been received or expended. It should also show any balances.

Budgeting

The Budgeting process is one of the most important and fundamental aspects of municipal administration. Maine Law (30 MRSA §5101-12) states that every municipality shall submit and adopt a budget yearly.

The two different budgeting processes being used throughout the State of Maine are "Net Budgeting" and "Gross Budgeting". Many of the smaller communities, throughout the state are still using a "Net Budgeting Process". This process consists of:

1. Subtracting non-tax anticipated sources of revenue from the estimated cost of the municipal function being performed.
2. Dedicating certain revenues only for specific activities.
3. Carrying over certain "Open Account Balances" from one Fiscal Year to another.

With "Net Budgeting", the focus is more on the "Amount to be Raised by Taxation", rather than on the "Total Expenditure". It is difficult to provide full accountability of the revenues and expenditures using this process. A larger Departmental Budget can have a smaller amount to be raised by taxation if Management uses more revenues and balances carried than a smaller departmental budget that is only funded by taxes. The focus should be on the total expenditures and not only on the amount to be raised by taxes. Sometimes, in "Net Budgeting" the total expenditures are not appropriated.

Gross Budgeting focuses on the total expenditures and the total estimated revenues. The revenues are budgeted separately and a separate article is developed to appropriate all the revenues to be used to reduce the amount to be raised by taxation. Balances that are left over at the end of the year are allowed to lapse into the Undesignated Fund Balance. A portion of the Undesignated Fund Balance may be used to reduce the amount to be raised by taxation. The only time that a balance would be carried over to the next Fiscal Year would be, if it was part of designated revenue, that was being used to fund a particular expenditure and not all of the revenue was used to cover the expenditures. An example might be in the use of a state or federal grant that restricted the use of those particular funds. The amount to be appropriated would be the total expenditures for that account.

When budgeting revenues, all the revenues received in the prior years need to be reviewed and analyzed to see if there are any abnormalities. The effect of the economy should also to be taken into consideration. If the economy has taken a downturn, there may be less state or federal funding, excise taxes and town clerk fees.

A portion of the Undesignated Fund Balance may be used to reduce the amount to be raised by taxes or may be used to offset certain capital expenditures in the budget. How much to be used depends on how much is in the fund. A "rule of thumb" for determining the amount to be retained in the fund is to have a minimum of 10% of the total gross budget (Total Appropriations). Some accountants recommend maintaining 8-24% for Cash Flow purposes and for emergencies that may come up after going to Commitment.

Another source of funding might be certain designated Reserve Funds that have been set up for special purposes.

One thing that must be remembered is that all expenditures and all revenues must be appropriated. When the Town Meeting votes to appropriate, it is authorizing the expenditure of funds and the use of certain revenues. An article should to be inserted in the Town Meeting Warrant that appropriates all of the revenues, balances carried and the amount of undesignated fund balance that are to be used to reduce the amount to be raised by taxation.

A budget schedule should be developed and issued approximately 4 months prior to the Annual Town Meeting. Along with the budget schedule, it is important for the Municipal Officers to establish budget goals for the coming year. This provides a guideline for everyone to follow in developing his or her budgets. If, in developing their budget, a department head or committee chairperson finds it necessary to exceed the established goal set by the Municipal Officers, they should provide the reasons why in writing. Copies of the current and prior years budgeted expenses and actual expenditures should be provided to each department head and committee chairperson to help them in the development of their proposed budget. Standard budget forms may be used as a part of the budget process.

Once the budgets have been completed, they should be submitted to the Municipal Officers. The Municipal Officers will review the budgets and draft the articles for the Town Meeting that will appropriate the funds for the overall budgets. The articles and the proposed budgets are then submitted to the Warrant & Finance (Budget) Committee for their review and recommendation.

When the Warrant & Finance (Budget) committee has completed their review and made their recommendation on all of the articles, the Municipal Officers will complete the warrant and send it to the printers. The warrant must be posted at least 7 days prior to the Town Meeting. The date to start the 7 day posting may be different from the actual date of the town meeting, where everybody assembles to vote on the overall town meeting warrant. If elections of municipal officials or referendum questions, to be voted on by "Secret Ballot" are held prior to the general voting on the general town meeting articles, the date to be used for purposes of the posting would be the date that the date that the elections or referendums take place.

Copies of both the Expense Budget and the Revenue Budget should be provided along with the Town Meeting Warrant, so that the townspeople have a better knowledge of what they are voting for when they vote on the separate articles. These budgets usually show both this year's and last year's figures.

Audits

Maine Law (30 MRSA section 5233) requires that each Municipality have an Annual Post-Audit made of its accounts covering the last complete Fiscal Year. Approximately two months, prior to the end of the Fiscal Year, the Municipal Officers need to decide whether to renew the contract for doing the Annual Audit or whether to go out with a Notice of Request for Proposal (RFP) for the Annual Audit. The RFP should include a deadline for completion of the Audit. The audit should be completed prior to going to commitment to ensure that any Prior Years Figures, used in determining the commitment, are accurate.

The Year-End work is very closely related to the work of the Auditors and should be coordinated with them as much as possible. It is advisable to meet with the Auditors prior to the years end and have them help in making up a checklist of items that the auditors will require in the conduct of their Audit and to assist in the proper closing of the Towns Books.

Be sure that the audit report contains a breakdown of the "Designated Fund Balances". The breakdown should contain all of the "Balances Carried" to the next Fiscal Year. It is important for the Municipal Officers to understand what the various figures mean in the audit report. They need to take seriously the comments and recommendations of the auditor and be willing to implement any recommendations. The audit can be a very useful and effective tool in improving the management of the municipal finances of the community.

Care should be exercised in choosing an Auditor. Price alone should not determine the selection of an Auditor. Experience in Municipal Accounting/Audit is a very important factor that should be taken into consideration in the evaluation process. It should be remembered that the Auditor works for and reports to the Municipal Officers and not the staff.

Example (1) is a sample of a "Notice of Request for Proposal for Annual Audit" and Example (2) is a sample "RFP for Annual Independent Audit".

Example (1): Notice of Request for Proposal

NOTICE OF REQUEST FOR

PROPOSALS FOR ANNUAL INDEPENDENT AUDIT

The Town of **NAME OF TOWN**, Maine will receive sealed proposals for ANNUAL INDEPENDENT AUDIT services until **INSERT TIME A.M./P.M.** on **INSERT DAY, INSERT DATE** at the **INSERT NAME OF OFFICE AND ADDRESS**, Maine at which time and place all proposals will be publicly opened and read aloud. Contract documents, specifications and the Request for Proposals are on file at the **INSERT NAME OF OFFICE AND ADDRESS, TELEPHONE NUMBER**.

Date: _____

Town of **INSERT NAME**, Maine

By: _____
INSERT AUTHORIZED SIGNATURE

Example (2): Request for Proposal

REQUEST FOR PROPOSALS

ANNUAL INDEPENDENT AUDIT

The Town of **INSERT NAME**, Maine invites qualified independent public accountants to submit proposals for the performance of an audit of its financial accounts and records covering the period **INSERT DATE** through **INSERT DATE**, for the purpose of rendering an auditor's opinion regarding the fairness of applicable financial statements and the compliance of the municipality with applicable legal provisions, in accordance with generally accepted auditing standards.

A. GENERAL INFORMATION

INSERT GENERAL INFORMATION (TYPE OF RECORD KEEPING SYSTEM, SIZE OF BUDGET, POPULATION ETC.)

B. AUDIT SPECIFICATIONS

Indicate in the proposal if the firm agrees to meet the following specifications. Explain any exceptions.

1. The audit firm shall be engaged to conduct a financial and compliance audit of the accounts, records and procedures of all departments, funds, account groups and/or entities of the municipality as stated in Section A of the Request for Proposal.
2. This examination shall be made in accordance with generally accepted auditing standards and procedures, applicable to governmental units, as prescribed in the following documents:
   a. American Institute of Certified Public Accountants, Statements on Auditing Standards and <u>Audits of State and Local Governmental units</u>.
   b. United States General Accounting Office, <u>Statements of Audit of Governmental Organizations, Programs, Activities and</u> Functions and Guidelines for Financial and <u>Compliance Audits of Federally Assisted</u> Programs.
3. The audit shall be conducted to satisfy the requirements the State of Maine Department of Audit and Title 30-a M.R.S.A., Section 5823. The firm shall also file the Municipal Audit Procedural Form and a copy of the auditor's report with the State Department of Audit within thirty days after completion of the Audit.
4. The firm shall submit a written report containing an expression of opinion that the financial statements are fairly stated, or if a qualified or adverse opinion or disclaimer of opinion is necessary, the reasons therefore. The firm shall submit **INSERT NUMBER** copies of the final draft of its report no later than **INSERT DATE** days after the close of the Fiscal Year.
5. In connection with the examination of the records and financial statements, the Firm shall review the system of internal control, operating procedures and compliance with budgetary and legal requirements by the municipality.

6. The firm shall agree to make available its working papers upon request to meet any municipal financial needs, as well as in accordance with any federal and state grant provisions.

7. Staff involved with the audit must have the appropriate certification, training, background and experience to perform the audit according to the rules and regulations of the Single Audit Act and the audit process shall be conducted in conformance with the Single Audit Act.

8. The partner or manager in charge of the audit shall be available to attend public meetings at which the auditor's report may be discussed. The partner or manager in charge of the audit shall also be available to discuss the auditor's report or other reports required by this proposal with the municipality's financial staff as required.

9. The municipality views its engagement of an audit as an ongoing professional relationship in which the firm is expected to provide consultation services during the terms of their proposal. As such, the firm is expected to consult as required on auditing, accounting, financial reporting and other financial management questions, which arise during the course of the year.

C. INSTRUCTION FOR SUBMITTING

Six copies of the proposal will be accepted in sealed envelopes marked "Independent Audit Proposal" until **INSERT TIME** on **INSERT DAY, INSERT DATE**.

In order to obtain uniform evaluation and maximum comparability, the proposal must be organized in the following manner:

1. Title Page

   The Title Page should reference the RFP subject and name of the municipality, the firm's name, address, and telephone number, the date, and the name and title of the contact person.

2. Table of Contents

   The Table of Contents must clearly identify the organization of the proposal by sections and include page numbers for easy reference.

3. Letter of Transmittal

   The letter should state the firm's understanding of the scope of the audit and contain a firm commitment to meet the audit specifications contained in Section II within the proper time period(s).

   In addition, the letter should identify the name of the person who will be authorized to make a representation for the firm and include that person's title, address and phone number.

4. Qualifications of the Firm

   This section must include all relevant information to assist the municipality in evaluating the firm's qualifications and experience in conducting municipal audits. The proposal must include at minimum:

   a. General Profile

   Information included should state whether the firm is local, regional or national, give the location of the office from which audit is to be conducted, the number and positions of the various professional staff located at that office, and describe the range of services performed by that office, such as audit, accounting, tax and management services.

    b. Staff Qualifications

The next section of the proposal must identify specifically who will be assigned to the audit, such as partner, manager, and supervisor. Resumes for each person assigned to the audit should be included.

    c. Relevant Experience

This section should describe the firm's municipal auditing experience including names and phone numbers of municipal officials responsible for the audits that can be contacted for more information.

5. Technical Approach

The proposal must include a summary of the firm's technical approach to performing a municipal audit. The proposal should include a brief description of the audit procedures and/or techniques to be followed, presented in a form which shall best aid the municipality in evaluating your firm's ability to identify, evaluate and communicate on local government financial problems.

6. Compensation

The proposal must indicate the maximum total fee your firm will charge for the audit services outlined in Section B of this Request for Proposal. The final payment shall become due only after the submission of all reports required by Section B and their acceptance by the municipality. Should the firm encounter circumstances requiring an increase on the extent of detailed investigation, or should the municipality require an increase in the scope of the audit, written notice to the effect must be given to the other party. The engagement can then be modified by mutual agreement of both practices as to additional work and compensation.

D. MUNICIPAL ASSISTANCE

The municipality's staff shall render all feasible assistance to the audit firm and shall respond promptly to requests for information, provide all necessary books and records, and provide physical facilities required by the firm for the expeditious conduct of the audit engagement.

The municipality shall have adjusted and/or closed all accounts and shall have them available for examination within **INSERT NUMBER OF** days after the close of the Fiscal Year. The municipality will also make its records and other financial documents available prior to the end of the Fiscal Year so that the firm may begin its preliminary work well before the close of the Fiscal Year, in order to complete the audit report on a timely basis.

E. EVALUATION OF PROPOSALS

The municipality shall evaluate the proposals on the basis of the qualifications, experience and responsiveness of the audit firms, as well as the estimated cost of the engagement. The municipality must be satisfied that the auditors and their firm have solid understanding of government programs generally and the operations of the municipality in particular.

The municipality may wish to conduct oral interviews with the firms considered most qualified in order to assist the municipality in the selection process. The municipality reserves the right to except any proposal, or reject any or all proposals, if it feels it is in the best interest of the municipality to do so.

F.   FURTHER INFORMATION

Audit firms who want additional information or clarification should contact the municipality. Any inquiries should be directed to **INSERT NAME, TITLE, INSERT ADDRESS AND TELEPHONE NUMBER**

Cash Flow Analysis

At the beginning of the Fiscal Year, the Treasurer should create a "Cash Flow Analysis" of the cash that is available throughout the coming year to pay all the bills and payroll. The bulk of the cash available comes from the receipt of real estate taxes and personal property taxes. Those municipalities sending tax bills out once a year will find that there will not be enough revenues available to carry them throughout the year. Even those municipalities that have gone to twice a year tax billing may find that they may run out of cash if they do not carry the recommended amount of Undesignated Fund Balance".

By creating a cash flow analysis, the Municipal Officers can anticipate the need for a Tax Anticipated Note (TAN). This is a short-term note that the town repays as the tax receivables come in.

The analysis starts by listing out the total estimated revenues and the total estimated expenditures on a monthly basis. The estimates are based on the prior year figures and modified by looking at the upcoming year's estimated revenues and expenditures. It is important to take into consideration any major expenditures or increases in the budget, which was authorized by the Town Meeting for the current year.

Beginning with the Cash Balance, available at the start of the Fiscal Year, the estimated Monthly Revenues are added and the Estimated Monthly Expenditures are subtracted, yielding a Net Cash Balance for that month. This is repeated for all twelve months. For any months that show a "Negative Cash Balance", an analyses needs to be made of the revenues and expenditures to see if any changes can be made. It may show that if the Tax Commitment had been made sooner, it would bring in some tax revenue sooner. Perhaps, there may be a large expenditure that could be delayed. If neither action is able to correct the situation, then it will be necessary to obtain a loan or a "Line of Credit from a Financial Institution. This generally happens just prior to Commitment and only requires a short-term loan, which would be paid off upon receipt of sufficient funds.

Rules for Financial Management of Municipal/School Funds

Years of experience have resulted in the compilation of the following rules that must be adhered to in order to maintain control over the budget.

1. All Expenditures and the use of Revenues must be authorized by the Town Meeting.
2. No accounts may be legally over-expended except for the Road/Highway Account and the General Assistance Account. An overdraft in the Road/Highway account may not exceed 15% of the appropriated amount and must have the written consent of the Selectmen. <u>All overdrafts must be ratified by the voters by the next Annual Town Meeting.</u> Appropriate actions should be taken to prevent the necessity of having to overdraft an account. MMA advises that Municipal Officers and in some cases the Treasurer may be held liable for any overdrafts that are not ratified by the Town Meeting. Allowing overdrafts is a sign of weakness of management in managing a departments budget. <u>Municipal Officers should be resolute in their commitment to not allow overdrafts.</u>
3. Within a specific appropriation, a subaccount may be over expended as long as the overall appropriation does not exceed what was voted by the Town Meeting for that article. This procedure is preferred over the transfer of funds from one subaccount to another. It is recommended that the Municipal Officers not allow the transfer of funds. The transfer of funds from one account to another must be authorized by the Town Meeting.
4. All funds to be carried over to the next Fiscal Year must be designated. (This is usually done with one Article listing all the funds to be carried over).
5. All undesignated funds and balances lapse into the Town's Undesignated Fund Balance (Surplus), except for undesignated school funds. Undesignated school funds and balances lapse into a School Undesignated Fund Balance Account for school purposes. It is recommended that the Undesignated Fund Balance be at least 10% of the total amount appropriated.
6. When designated revenues are used in the appropriation, there are strict limitations to their use. You are only allowed to use what is appropriated. If an appropriation consists of an estimated amount of $10,000 and you receive only $5,000, you must cut your budgeted expenditures by $5,000 for that account. If you receive $15,000 instead of $10,000 you cannot spend the extra $5,000 because it was not appropriated. If funds are received during the upcoming Fiscal Year that were not specifically appropriated then they cannot be used unless authorized by the Town Meeting. They may be carried forward or they will lapse into the Undesignated Fund Balance or into the School's Fund Balance.

   NOTE: The appropriations may only be increased if the new revenues have been appropriated by a Town Meeting Article. The use of **all** Revenues should be approved by the Town Meeting. These include all Revenues that are to be used to reduce taxes when figuring the Commitment.

Purchasing Guidelines

Having a set of policies and procedures is an important part of controlling municipal costs. The following is a set of purchasing guidelines used by the Town of _____.

Policy

It is the policy of the Town of _____ to make maximum use of Purchase Orders in the purchase of goods and services.

Purpose

The use of Purchase Orders will allow the Town to provide the best guarantees that tax money and public funds are spent in the most prudent fashion. It provides a full audit trail of purchases and is an important tool to help prevent overdrafts and control spending within budget limits.

Scope

The following procedures shall apply to all departments except the school department. The school department will use its own procedures for the use of Purchase Orders.

Responsibilities of the Purchasing Agent and Department Heads

An effective centralized purchasing system is based upon standard procedures being utilized by all departments on a consistent basis. These procedures must be clearly explained and communicated to all who are involved in the purchase of goods and services with public funds. Specific responsibilities for various aspects of purchasing are shared by the purchasing agent and department heads as follows:

Purchasing Agent Responsibilities:
NOTE: The ( ) is designated as the Purchasing Agent for the Town of _____.

A. Where departments are authorized to purchase directly from vendors (for example, under $200.00 in value), assist them in ensuring that procedures are followed.

B. Purchase all goods and services valued over $200.00 in total price, for the departments other than the school department, when requested.

C. Receives and reviews all Purchase orders (PO's) for availability of funds; enters PO into accounting system and processes PO.

D. Responsible for certifying the availability of funds before any purchase over $200.00 is made.

E. If the unencumbered balance in the appropriation account is insufficient, returns PO to the originating department with **NOTICE OF INSUFFICIENT FUNDS** attached.

F. Upon receipt of an invoice, the Purchasing Agent pulls PO from file and forwards to appropriate department head for authorization of payment and receiving report. Files office copy in "active" file.

G. Upon receipt of approval from department head, processes PO for payment; liquidates account encumbrance; enters all date in the computerized accounting system.

H. Upon receipt of vendor's invoice from department without an accompanying PO, return PO to department with attached notice of **NO PURCHASE ORDER**. If a purchase was made without an authorized PO issued by the Purchasing Agent, do not process for payment.

I. Prepare all contracts for execution, including any performance bonds, insurance certificates, labor and materials bonds, obtain the required signatures, distribute contract documents, and assign contract numbers to all contracts and agreements awarded by the municipality. He/She shall also maintain these files with any additional documents or correspondence relating to contracts or agreements. Purchasing files will contain all material associated with the planning, bidding, and acquisition of the product or service.

J. Supervise and maintain control of any storerooms or other facilities for the storage or distribution of supplies for any two or more departments/offices.

K. Coordinate with the school department for consolidated purchases of common items such as paper goods, fuel oil, etc.

L. Compile and maintain lists of prospective vendors of supplies and services and invite bids and proposals from such vendors.

M. Maintain bid files and other documents. Note that certain vendor files containing some confidential vendor business information is not considered open to the public, particularly financial information needed for qualifications analysis, but not for public review.

Department Head Responsibilities:

A. For purchases up to the minimum amount (for example $200.00 in total value), to purchase goods and services for the orderly and efficient operation of their departments within the appropriated budget.

B. Work cooperatively with the Purchasing Agent within the purchasing system to ensure the best interests of the municipality and its departments are met.

C. Anticipate the department's needs well in advance, so as to minimize the needs for emergency purchase.

D. Prepare item descriptions and specifications, so as to provide the vendor with a clear indication of the department's needs.

E. Upon receipt of goods or services, to review the Purchase Order and invoice for conformity. Attach receiving report to invoice.

F. When there is a discrepancy of cost or dissatisfaction with goods received, to notify the Purchasing Agent at once to resolve problem. No bill should be processed for payment where goods are unsatisfactory, or there is a price discrepancy between original Purchase Order and bill received.

Procedures

Purchases up to the Minimum Amount

Any purchases up to $200.00 may be made, without a PO, by the Department Head or an employee with the Department Head's concurrence. If the Town of Acton has a charge account with the particular store or vendor then the goods may be charged to the Town's account. If the Town does not have an account with a particular store or vendor then the employee may pay for the goods and apply for reimbursement from the Town using forms supplied by the Treasurer's Office.

Purchases from $200.00 TO $1000.00

Any purchases of goods or services from $200.00 to $1000.00 shall require the use of a regular Purchase Order Form:

A. The Department shall request the purchase on a Purchase Order form. This form shall be submitted to the Purchasing Agent by the requesting Department.
B. The Department Head or his designee shall contact as many venders as necessary in order to obtain at least three (3) written or verbal quotations.
C. The Department Head shall select the appropriate vendor. In exceptional circumstances, if the lowest quotation is not recommended, it must be indicated as attachments to the Purchase Order Form with full documentation and explanation to the Selectmen for approval.
D. Once filled out, the Purchase order will be forwarded to the Purchasing Agent for processing.
E. The Purchasing Agent will then certify as to the availability of funds and will execute the purchase if approved.

Purchases exceeding maximum amount

Purchases or contracts exceeding $1000.00 shall be by bid or Request for Proposal (RFP). Unless you have someone fully knowledgeable to write up the specifications for going out to bid, it is recommended that the "Request for Proposal" be used.

A. The Department Head shall prepare specifications for Bid/RFP items and shall obtain technical assistance as needed in interpreting and preparing certain specifications.
B. All Bid/RFP specifications must be approved as to form by the Board of Selectmen.
C. After approval of the purchase by the Selectmen, the Purchasing Agent shall invite all Bids/RFP's by advertisement in at least one newspaper of general circulation in the municipality, such publication to be at least one week before the time of Bid opening. A typical Bid/RFP invitation is shown below.

Sample Bid/RFP Notice

BID/RFP NOTICE

The Town of _____, Maine invites Bids/RFP for the supply of (name of bid item). Bid/RFP specifications are available from the Office of Selectmen, _____, Maine, 040__, Tel.___-____. Sealed Bids will be received until _____ AM/PM, (date), at which time Bids will be opened and publicly read. The Town reserves the right to reject any and all Bids/Proposals if deemed in the interest of the Town.

a. All Bids/RFP's shall be opened in public. Bids meeting the specifications shall be reviewed by the Selectmen in consultation with the Department Head or committee.

b. The Department Head or committee shall then make a bid award recommendation. If the Department Head or committee recommends that the lowest Bid be accepted and the Selectmen know of no extenuating circumstances, the Selectmen shall so award the Bid.

c. If there are extenuating circumstances felt by the Department Head, Committee or Selectmen, the Board of Selectmen may award the Bid to other than the lowest Bidder or may reject any or all Bids.

d. RFP's shall be reviewed for content and the ability to fulfill the requirements/specifications contained in the RFP as well as the price quoted.

e. At the direction of the Selectmen, the Purchasing Agent shall prepare a Notice of Award Form to be attached to the purchase order or contract.

Change Orders

Whenever a change of any kind occurs on the original purchase order, a new Purchase Order, with the updated information must be submitted by the department, modifying the Purchase Order. The modified order will be rerouted for approval with the notation as to "Modifying or Changing Purchase Order No._____".

Emergency Purchases

a. **General**

Although the occasion for emergency purchases will arise, this practice should be kept to a minimum by anticipating the department's needs well in advance and using the regular purchasing guidelines. The competitive procurement provisions can only be waived by the Selectmen for a purchase over the $1000.00 limit when there exists a special emergency involving the health or safety of the people or property. When an emergency purchase is made, the department doing so, or the Purchasing Agent will attempt to make the purchase at the most competitive price. An emergency generally relates to needed repairs to equipment or facilities which must be kept operating to protect the health and/or safety of persons, or property.

b. **Emergency Purchase Procedure**

If the need for any emergency purchase arises, the following procedure should be followed:

1) The Department Head or Purchasing Agent should prepare a Purchase order and give a clear explanation of the nature of the emergency in the "remarks" section. The Purchase Order should then be marked **"Emergency"**. Every effort shall be made to inform the Selectmen of the need for the purchase and obtain his/her approval. Attempts should be made to obtain competitive quotes, if possible.

2) This Purchase Order should be promptly forwarded to the Selectmen, regardless of dollar value. In the event that the emergency should occur when the Selectmen's Office is closed, the purchase may be made and the emergency Purchase Order submitted to the Selectmen as soon thereafter as possible.

3) Where the purchase price exceeds the unencumbered balance. In the Department's budget account, the Department shall immediately notify the Selectmen of the need. No purchase shall be completed prior to such notification and approval by the Selectmen.

Procedures for the Receipt of Supplies or Services

The following procedures shall be followed for the receipt of all supplies or services:

a. **Full Receipt of Shipment**

   The Department Head will notify the Purchasing Agent that supplies were received by signing the invoice and forwarding it to the Purchasing Agent.

b. **Partial Receipt of Shipment**

   If partial shipment of an order is received, the Department Head should note what remains to be received. The invoice or packing slip should also be noted that the order is incomplete and the Purchasing Agent should be notified.

c. **Inspection and Acceptance**

   The Department Head will be responsible for the inspection of supplies or services received. He will determine that the supplies or services are as specified and satisfactory before accepting same.

d. **Payment of Transportation Charges**

   All orders to suppliers will normally specify that transportation charges will be prepaid by the supplier to the point of delivery.

e. **Invoices Necessary**

   The person making the purchase will insure that the invoice is to the Town of Acton and should also insure that the vendor provides a legible and complete description of the item purchased on the invoice. A copy of the supplier's invoice signed by the person making the purchase will be delivered to the Department Head who shall verify the receipt of the item and insure that the invoice reflects the department and activity for which the purchase was made by signing the invoice. Invoices shall be delivered to the Purchasing Agent as soon as possible.

Investment Policy

Every Municipality should have an "Investment Policy. The following is an example that may be used:

"This investment policy applies to all transactions involving the Financial Assets of the Town of_____. The main objective is safety of Principal. Each investment transaction shall seek to ensure that Capital losses are avoided. Assets of the Town shall be invested only in Certificates of Deposit, Treasury Bills, and Treasury Bonds of the U.S. Government, Repurchase agreements with banks chartered by the State of Maine and Collateralized by U.S. Treasury Bills. The Treasurer shall only make investments as directed by the Board of Selectmen. Presently, all funds, except Trust Funds, are maintained in a single checking account with the _____Bank. The funds may be invested by the bank as part of a Cash Management Account where they are invested on a daily basis therefore providing interest income to the Town."

Capital Improvement Program (CIP)

General

1. In its most basic form, a CIP is no more than a schedule listing Capital Improvements, in order of priority, together with cost estimates and the proposed method of financing them.
2. A CIP provides the following benefits to the Community:
   a. Focuses attention on Community goals, needs and capabilities.
   b. Maintains a sound and stable Financial Management Program.
   c. Repairs or replaces existing facilities/equipment.
   d. Achieves optimum use of Taxpayers money.
   e. Enhances likelihood for Grant-in-Aid monies.
   f. Serves and informs the Public Interest in Projects.
3. Capital Improvement Projects must meet the following criteria:
   a. Total cost of no less than $3000.00—$5000.00. Items below this figure will normally be included in the Maintenance Account.
   b. Minimal useful life of three years.

Procedure

1. The Selectmen shall appoint a Capital Improvement Committee (CIC).
2. The CIC shall prepare a Capital Improvement Plan that meets the long-term needs of the Town. In preparing the CIP, the CIC will:
   a. Make an inventory of all the Municipal Assets.
   b. Determine the condition of the Assets.
   c. Determine the Useful Life of the Assets.
3. The CIC will also develop a list of any new proposed Capital Improvement Projects. The cost of each Capital Improvement shall be determined.
4. Once the list and costs have been determined, it will be necessary to establish a priority list for the proposed projects.
5. The plan or update of the plan should be presented to the Selectmen, along with recommendations for financing the improvements, in sufficient time so that it may be included with other Town Meeting Articles for the Annual Town Meeting.
6. In order to fund the proposed Capital Improvements, It will be necessary to establish a Capital Improvement Fund.

Commitment Process

Prior to starting the Commitment Process, it is important that the Annual Audit for the Prior year to have been completed. This is to ensure that any estimated balances from the prior year that have been authorized by the Annual Town Meeting, are in fact valid balances. All revenues and balances, to be used to reduce the amount to be raised by taxation, must be appropriated by the Town Meeting.

When considering the amount of Undesignated Fund Balance, to be used to reduce the amount to be used in the commitment process, consideration needs to be taken, as to how much is left in the Undesignated Fund Balance Account. The audit report should show the balance as of the end of the year. It is recommended that a minimum of 10% of the overall total budget be retained in the Undesignated Fund Balance to cover emergencies during the current year and to enhance the cash flow of the town.

Once all of the property valuations, as of April 1st of the prior year, have been entered into the computer, a cross check of the names and addresses should be done between the tax assessing files and the tax billing files. Any errors found should be corrected.

The following steps outline the procedure to be used by the Tax Assessors in the commitment of the Taxes to the Tax Collector:

1. Ensure that all the changes affecting assessed values (as of 1 April) are entered in the computer.
2. Run a "Commitment Verify Report" and check for any errors. Make Corrections as necessary.
3. Run a "Valuation Analysis" to obtain the Total Valuation for Real Estate and Personal Property.
4. Run a list of Homestead Exemptions to determine the amount of valuation due to the Homestead Exemption. Add this amount to the total valuation for use in determining the tax rate.
5. Ensure that all Appropriations have been entered into the Expense (Appropriation) Accounts.
6. On the Assessor's form used for the Municipal Tax Rate Calculation, the total expenses/ appropriations should be the same as the total expenses/appropriation on the expense/ appropriation control report. The total deductions should equal the estimated revenues, balances carried (if included in the expense/appropriation totals) and any Undesignated Fund Balance appropriated by the Town Meeting
7. Calculate the minimum and maximum tax rates. The minimum tax rate would be without using any overlay. The maximum overlay set by state statues is 5% over that amount needed to be raised by taxes. It is recommended that a minimum amount be chosen to round off the tax rate, but should, also be enough to cover the amount of abatements estimated for the current tax year. Too much Overlay only increases the tax rate unnecessarily.
8. After determining the amount of overlay, calculate the tax rate and the total taxes to be committed.
9. Fill out the commitment sheets to the Tax Collector and Treasurer.
10. Run a Trial Commitment on green bar paper, if okay, and then run a Final Commitment using 2 part commitment paper.
11. Determine the percentage of total taxes (excluding overlay) for the County Taxes, Municipal Taxes and School Taxes. Then, using the percentages, determine the portion of the overall mil rate that will be used for the County Taxes, the Municipal Appropriations and the School Appropriations.
12. Determine the percent that the Tax Bill would have increased without State Aid for Education and State Revenue Sharing.

13. Provide the Commitment and other appropriate information, as determined in the previous steps, to the Tax Collector and Treasurer. A copy should be retained for the Selectmen/ Assessor's Files.
14. Once the Commitment has been verified, a separate backup should be set up to off load only the R.E. and P.P. Files, and this labeled "20XX Tax Commitment Files". Continue to use the correct backup for the day to day backups.
15. After the commitment has been entered in the General Ledger by the Tax Collector, it will be transferred to the Revenue Account (property taxes-assessed) in YTD receipts. From the "Municipal Tax Rate Calculation Form" take the "net to be raised by Local Tax Rate" and enter this in the Revenue Account (property taxes-assessed) as Estimated Receipts.

Tax Collection

Once the taxes have been committed by the Assessors, the Tax Collector becomes legally responsible for the collection of those taxes within the time period stated in the tax commitment and is required to exhaust all legal avenues available for collection. The Tax Collectors & Treasurers Manual put out by MMA provides various procedures that may be used in the collection of taxes. The Tax Collector shall exhibit to the Board of Selectmen, an account of all the monies received on taxes committed to him or her, at least once every two months.

Tax Settlement and Discharge

Upon completion of collection of taxes for a given year, the Tax Collector shall prepare a "Certificate of Settlement" (Example3) and present it to the Selectmen for approval. The certificate shall be accompanied by appropriate supporting documents.

After the Selectmen have had a reasonable opportunity to review the statement and supporting documents, they will indicate their approval of the figures as presented by signing the discharge of liability at the bottom of the certificate. This action should be taken at a regularly scheduled Selectmen's meeting.

Once the certificate is signed, the Tax Collector is free of liability for the collection of any remaining balance of taxes for that year.

Example 3: Certificate of Settlement and Discharge

STATE OF MAINE

COUNTY OF_____ss.

TO_____, Tax Collector of the Municipality of _____within this county:

  We hereby certify that the 20_____ taxes committed to you consisting of:

1. Real and Personal Tax Commitments: $_____

2. Supplemental Commitments Totaling: $_____

3. Interest: $_____
4. A Grand Total of: $_____

5. Cash Payments: $_____

6. Abatements Granted: $_____

7. Tax Lien Mortgages: $_____
(Recorded in the_____County Registry of Deeds)

8. Other Credits: $_____

9. A Net Total Of: $_____

10. Balance Due Of: $_____

Under the authority contained in MRSA, Title 36, Section 736, as amended, we hereby discharge you from further liability or obligation to collect the balance due of:

  $_____ and acknowledge receipt of the tax lists for the taxable year 20_____.

Given under our hands this_____day of_____A.D. 20_____.

                                                                Municipal Officers:

                                                _____

Certificate of Settlement and Discharge Instructions

USE A SEPARATE FORM FOR EACH COMMITMENT YEAR.

EXECUTE IN TRIPLICATE (one each for tax collector, municipal records, and the bondsman).

Line 1-4.—Enter total commitments for the single taxable year, i.e., personal, real and supplemental taxes. Interest paid on taxes after the due date is entered on line 4 and line 8. Do not use commitments of other years. Use separate form for recommitted taxes of previous years.

Line 5.—Enter cash collections supported by treasurer's receipts.

Line 6.—Enter abatements granted to the taxpayer or the tax collector according to the assessors' records.

Line 7.—Enter only recorded tax lien mortgage sums. Do not enter unrecorded liens of tax collector's deeds. Do not credit unrecorded liens on this form.

Line 8.—Include here such items as tax deeds, discounts for early payment, suits brought in the name of the Municipality, interest, etc.

Line 9.—Total of lines 5 through 9.

Line 10.—Subtract line 9 from line 4.

What affects the Tax Rate?

Essentially, the Tax Rate is determined by dividing the Commitment by the Taxable Valuation.

> **Example**: Taxable Valuation = $500,000,000
> Commitment = $5,000,000
>
> **Tax Rate** = $\dfrac{\$5,000,000}{\$500,000,000}$ = .010 or $10.00/$1000

The following parameters have an effect on the Tax Rate:

> **Valuation:** For each $1,000,000 increase in Taxable Valuation, there will be only a $.02 decrease in the Tax Rate.
>
> **Commitment**: For every $100,000 increase in the Commitment, there will be an increase of $.20 in the Tax Rate.

Note: The increase/decrease in the Tax Rate is representative only. The actual amount of increase/decrease will be dependent on the Actual Valuations or Commitment used.

What affects the Commitment?

(1) Appropriations
(2) Revenues
(3) Balances Carried (if included in the appropriations)
(4) Amount of Undesignated Fund Balance to be used to reduce Taxes
(5) Homestead Exemption
(6) Overlay

Comments

The major factor affecting the Commitment is Appropriations. Any significant increase in the Appropriations will need to be offset by increased Revenues or more utilization of the Undesignated Fund Balance.

Revenues do not vary that much from year to year, but are an integral part of the process in reducing the amount to be raised by taxation.

If a Gross Budgeting Process is used, the Balances Carried are a very minor item. In the Gross Budgeting Process, most of the balances are allowed to lapse into the Undesignated Fund Balance where they can be applied to the amount to be used to reduce the Commitment. Note: List the Balances Carried only if they were included in the appropriations)

In determining the amount of Undesignated Fund Balance, to be used in reducing the Commitment, it is recommended that 10% of the Total Appropriations or 15% of the Commitment be retained for Cash Flow purposes and to be available for emergencies.

The Homestead Exemption is fairly constant and any changes will only have a minor effect on the Commitment.

In determining Overlay, state statues allow a maximum of 5% of the Commitment, to be added and no less than 0%. It is recommended that a minimal amount be used, that can be used to round off the Tax Rate and be used for offsetting any abatements issued. Using too much Overlay only increases the Tax Rate unnecessarily.

Town Meeting Articles (involving Funding)

Town Meeting Articles, involving Funding, are written in a variety of ways. One of the older ways is:

"To see what sum the Town will vote to raise and/or appropriate for _____."

According to MMA, the problem with this is, that by not having any amount in the article itself, it leaves the total amount open ended. The motion on the floor may overwrite the figure that is recommended by the finance committee or the selectmen. A motion on the floor may, also, be amended to increase the amount. Articles written in this manner have no upper limit.

It is preferred to include a definite amount in the body of the article, such as "To see if the Town will raise and/or appropriate $ XXX for _____. By having a set figure in the body of the article, it sets an upper limit for what can be appropriated. You can not increase the figure listed in the article. The main thing to remember is to include the word "appropriate" in all articles pertaining to funding. The definition of "appropriate" is to authorize. The Town Meeting needs to "appropriate" (authorize) all expenditures and the use of all revenues.

Some towns appropriate the total amount, requested in each article. The total appropriations approved by the Town Meeting then become the total appropriations listed in the Commitment. A separate article is written to appropriate the total revenue and balances to be used to offset the amount to be raised by taxation. An example of this type of article is:

"To see if the Town will appropriate the following revenues and fund balances to cover the expenditures appropriated in the previous articles: (The remaining funding is to be raised by taxation.)

Estimated FY ( ) Municipal Revenues	$ XXXX *
Capital Improvement Fund	$ XXXX
Undesignated Fund Balance	$ XXXX
* (This figure is determined during the initial budget process.)	

I find that this method to be much cleaner and clearer when doing the Commitment. You can compare the total appropriations and the total revenues used in the commitment to what was appropriated by the Town Meeting.

When it is necessary to borrow money to finance an item or service, a financial statement concerning the amount of the town's debt is required to be included with the article in accordance with MRSA 30A, § 5404(1-A) & 5772(2-A). An example may be found in the appendices of the "Municipal Officer's Manual".

Chart of Accounts

Many small communities still use a simplified chart of accounts that have been passed on over the years. Most small town treasurers and selectmen have very limited training or knowledge on municipal accounting. For these towns, their chart of accounts may not be arranged in the format recommended by the Government Finance Officers Association (GFOA). Much of the auditor's time in doing the Annual Audit is spent trying to get the town's data into the format used by the auditor. In 2006, the Maine State Legislature enacted a resolve for the Department of Audit to develop a "Model Chart of Accounts". A committee was formed in the summer of 2006 to develop the Model Chart of Accounts. In 2007, an Act was passed by the 123rd Legislature to improve the access to Chart of Accounts. This Act required that the Model Chart of Accounts be made available on the Department of Audit's website [www.maine.gov/audit/], for access for all Municipal and County

Governments. The Act did not make the use mandatory, but may be used voluntarily by any level of government.

Note: Overlay is listed as an "Expense Account" (account 50930) in the Model Chart of Accounts. Overlay is not an expense, but, by definition, is part of the taxes to be raised and therefore a Revenue and is actually part of the Commitment. Overlay is not, normally, considered as part of the Budget Process and should not be listed as an "Expense Account".

Chapter 3

Assessing Guidelines

Assessing Guidelines

In many small towns in Maine, the elected Board of Selectmen serves also, as the elected Board of Assessors. It is highly recommended that all assessors receive basic training in assessing. The Department of Revenue Services puts on a training course every year, around the first week in August plus other training sessions throughout the year.

The Board of Assessors may contract out to an outside assessing firm for assistance in the performance of some of the assessing functions. This may be done, when the town has to do a complete revaluation or to help with the annual maintenance services.

It is important to remember that the contracted assessor, employed by the town, for the purpose of appraising property values, is not the town assessor, unless expressly appointed by the Board of Selectmen, pursuant to 30-A MRSA §2526. The contracted appraiser only provides information to the assessors, which may or may not be used in determining the actual assessments. For this reason, it is important that the assessors be knowledgeable of the methods used by the appraiser.

Board of Assessors Responsibilities

In general, the Board of Assessors has the following basic responsibilities:

Maintaining an updated mapping system, depicting all parcels of land in the community. This requires a review of all deed transfers, so that any subdivision of lots may be recorded on the tax maps and that proper square footage or acreage of the lots may be recorded.

Maintaining updated lists of all real and personal property so that taxes may be assessed to the owner of record.

Maintaining an updated record of all property exemptions, such as "Homestead", "Veteran" and "Blind".

Performing field inspections to determine pertinent data concerning the land, buildings, structures, equipment and any other improvements. A review of all building permits and plumbing permits will help to identify which properties need to be inspected for revaluation.

Determining property value. After collecting general, specific and comparative data on all types of property, the assessor analyzes the data and processes them into indications of value for each individual piece of property. The property is then assessed at its fair market value or some fraction thereof, known as the assessed value.

Determining the classification of all land and properties into their proper categories. This includes "tree growth", "farmland", "open space", shore land", "resource protection", general purpose and various exemptions.

Updating the assessing records with changes of ownership, changes of address, etc.

Maintaining and certifying the official Valuation Book/Records and subsequently determining the Tax Rate and Tax Commitment.

Reviewing all requests for abatements and taking the necessary action to approve or deny any abatements.

Representing the Town of _____ during any public hearings of the Board of Assessment Review.

Making supplemental assessments. At times, certain additional or supplemental assessments may be necessary where properties were inadvertently omitted from the regular assessment.

Notifying property owners of any changes in valuation.

Log Book

It is recommended that an Assessor's Log Book be established to record any changes to a property owner's assessment. There should be a separate log for each property owner in which there is a change in assessment. (See a sample 'Assessor's Log" at the end of the chapter). The Log should include the following information:

Map/Lot
Owner's Name
Amount of Adjustment
Reason for the adjustment
Name/Initials of the Assessor's Agent recommending the change
Date of Site Visit
Names of the two Assessors that approved the Valuation Adjustment
Date of Approval

The log book should be updated to reflect any of the following changes to a property owner's assessment:

Valuation Adjustments

All valuation adjustments must be verified by a site visit and recorded in the "Assessor's Log Book" and the "Property Record Card". Upon approval of a valuation adjustment, the property owner shall be notified in writing of the amount of the adjustment and the reason for it.

Abatements

All requests for abatements must be approved/denied by at least two of the assessors. If the Assessor's Agent is asked to make a recommendation on an abatement, the recommendation will be recorded in the Assessor's Log Book with the date, amount recommended and the name of the Assessor's Agent. The Property Record Card shall also be properly annotated to show the date of approval of the abatement.

Supplemental Assessments

When Supplemental Assessments are made, they will be recorded in the Assessor's Log Book and the Property Record Card in the same way as the Abatements.

All Supplemental Assessments should be approved by at least two of the assessors

<u>Property Record Cards</u>

The Property Record Cards may be Hard copies or stored digitally in an Assessing Program. Any Valuation Adjustments made shall be recorded on the Property Record Card with the amount of adjustment, reason for the adjustment, date of site visit and the initials of the person making the adjustment.

Town of _____ Assessor's Log (Sample)

Date:_____

Map/Lot:_____

Name of the Property Owner:_____

Valuation Adjustment: Yes/No Land:_____ Building:____

Amount of Adjustment:_____

Reason for the Adjustment:

Was a site visit made? Yes/No Date of site visit:_____

Name/Initials of the person recommending the adjustment:_____

Has the Property Record card been properly annotated? Yes/No

Names of two Assessors that have approved the Valuation Adjustment:

_____

_____

Date of approval:_____

Has the property owner been notified? Yes/No

Date of Notification:_____

Abatement requested: Yes/No

Was the Abatement: Approved/Denied

Was a Supplemental Assessment issued? Yes/No

Date of issue:_____

Chapter 4

<u>Municipal Management</u>

There have been many factors during the past 20 years that have changed the way of managing the small communities throughout rural Maine. Increased demand for services has created larger budgets and increased the amount of support staff. In addition, there are more State and Federal regulations. For towns that are still being managed by a part-time Board of Selectmen, the demands and pressures can be over-whelming. Whether your town is being managed by a Board of Selectmen, a Town Manager or an Administrative Assistant, the following list of attributes and actions can be important for the effective management of your community:

- Knowing your job. Learn your responsibilities and be committed to fulfill those responsibilities.
- Be willing to provide the time to attend training sessions to become a better and more effective manager.
- Be willing to ask for and accept help, when offered.
- Be willing to make the hard decisions for the betterment of the town. Remember, you may not be able to please everyone with your decision.
- Be willing to delegate tasks to others.
- Make sure you follow through when action items are brought to your attention. Do not procrastinate.
- Be a Leader and not a Follower. Do not wait for others to remind or tell you that certain things need to be done.
- Be tolerant and respectful of others. You may not agree with someone else's opinion or recommendation, however, be willing to listen.
- Be honest and straightforward. Do not say one thing and do another.
- If you say you are going to do something, then make sure you follow through and do it. Say what you mean, mean what you say, and do what you say you're going to do.
- Make sure you provide the public with the opportunity to ask questions or provide comments at your weekly Selectmen meetings.
- Be willing to admit that you were wrong, if you were. We are all human and subject to making mistakes.
- At the beginning of the Fiscal Year, establish a "Strategic Plan". List the problems facing your community and prepare a plan with actions and a schedule for implementing those actions.

- At the beginning of the new Fiscal Year, prepare a "Calendar of Events" for all the key events in the coming year. Review it on a weekly basis and add any new events as you become aware of them. This can be a great organizational tool to ensure that things get completed on time.
- Provide proper oversight of your departments and committees by scheduling periodic meetings with department heads and committee chairpersons.
- Maintain a "To-Do list". Do not let problems linger.
- Ensure that all of your employees have up-to-date job descriptions and make sure they are reviewed annually.
- Make certain you have a comprehensive "Personnel Policy".
- Ensure that a copy of all ordinances, policies and procedures are readily available to the public. They need to be reviewed annually to make sure they are current.
- Hold all employees and appointees accountable for their actions and for fulfillment of their responsibilities.
- Provide recognition for "Exemplary Work or Service".
- If your community has a website, make sure it is current and has accurate information.
- Become knowledgeable of the basics of "Municipal Accounting". You must be able to read and understand the various financial reports such as Expense Reports, Revenue Reports, General Ledger Trial Balance and Audit Reports.
- Become fully knowledgeable of the "Budget Process". This starts with a Budget Schedule, followed by Budget Preparation, Budget Execution and monitoring of the budget to make sure "overdrafts" are kept to an absolute minimum.
- Make certain the TC/TC and Treasurer provide you with Monthly Financial Reports.
- Make sure your community has a "Financial Policy and Procedures Manual".

Chapter 5

Decision Making/Selection Process

In managing a small community, many decisions have to be made. In having to make these decisions, it is important to have a formal process in place to document the rationale in making the decision and it also helps to remove or reduce any personal biases. It is especially important in the selection of personnel, but can be used in the selection of a company, contractor or other proposal being considered.

A simple process that can be used is as follows:

1. Make up a matrix listing the attributes that you feel are essential for the product, process, proposal or position that you are considering.
2. Prioritize the attributes and assign a weight to each attribute (1-5).
3. Establish your review questions so that you can evaluate the performance/qualifications against each attribute.
4. Based on the review, background data and other possible inputs rate each attribute on a scale from 0 to 5
5. When completed, multiply each rated score by the weight of the attribute.
6. Add up all the weighted scores for an overall score for that particular proposal or candidate.

Repeat this process for each proposal. The proposal or candidate with the highest score should be the one most qualified or best choice.

If there are multiple members of the selection panel, each member rates each proposal or candidate separately. When completed, add the final scores for each proposal or candidate and the one with the highest score should be the one most qualified or best choice.

Discuss the outcome with each member of the selection panel to ensure that the right choice is being made for the proposal or candidate. Remember, this process should help to remove any personal biases or prejudices that might influence the selection. If there is a major discomfit with the outcome, look at the attributes and their weights to ensure that everyone is comfortable with them as they pertain to the proposal or candidate. Do not revise things to validate any personal bias or prejudices.

Chapter 6

Code of Ethics

There is very little in the State of Maine statues concerning ethics. Title 30-A, §2605. par.7 states that "In their discretion, Municipal Officers may adopt an "Ethics Policy governing the conduct of elected and appointed officials.".". Every community should have an ethics policy or code of ethics that would apply to all elected and appointed officials. I have drafted the following Code of Ethics and highly recommend that every community adopt it or a variation of it:

(Sample Code of Ethics)

Code of Ethics and Conduct for Elected and Appointed Officials of the Town of _____

Preamble

The proper operation of the Town of _____ requires that all elected and appointed officials be honest, fair and impartial. They are responsible to the citizens and the citizens must have confidence in the integrity of the leaders of our community.

In recognition of these goals, there is hereby established a "Code of Ethics and Conduct" for all elected and appointed officials. The purpose of this document is to establish ethical standards of conduct for all such officials by setting forth guidelines for addressing those acts or actions that are incompatible with the best interests of the Town of Acton.

1. DEFINITIONS
For purposes of this document, the following terms shall have the meanings specified:
a. Officials—Any elected or appointed official of the Town of _____.
   a. Private advantage/benefit/gain—As used in this document, means any personal advantage, benefit or economic gain, distinct from that enjoyed by members of the general public without regard to the official status or not resulting from lawful and proper performance of duties.
   b. Community/Municipal—refers to the Town of _____.

46

c. Ethical Behavior—Ethics not only pertains to legal responsibilities, but also includes moral values such as honesty, impartiality and fairness.

2. AVOIDANCE OF IMPRESSIONS OF CORRUPTIBILITY

a. Officials shall conduct their duties so as not to give a reasonable basis for the impression that such official can be improperly influenced in the performance of his/her official duties. Such officials should conduct themselves so as to maintain public confidence in their performance and the community they represent. They should not be a source of embarrassment to the community and should avoid even the appearance of conflict in the conduct of their municipal duties.

3. IMPROPER ACTIVITIES

No official shall engage in any enterprise or activity which shall result in the following:

a. Using the prestige/influence of his/her office for private gain or advantage to himself/herself or another.

b. Using facilities, equipment or supplies of the municipality for personal gain or advantage for himself/herself or another.

c. Using official information not available to the public for his/her private gain or advantage or that of another.

d. Receiving or accepting, directly or indirectly, any gift or favor from anyone doing business with the municipality under circumstances from which it reasonably could be inferred that such was intended to influence him/her in the performance of his/her official duties, or as a reward for official action.

e. Knowingly, deviating from or ignoring local ordinances/procedures, state and federal laws.

f. Sanctioning unethical behavior of other municipal employees.

g. Use of disparaging remarks, ridicule, slurs, offensive jokes or other derogatory actions directed against another person.

h. Actions that may be considered intimidating, insulting, coercive or harassing behavior.

4. IMPROPER USE OF OFFICIAL POSITION

a. No municipal official shall use his/her position or the power or authority of his/her office or position in any manner intended to induce or coerce any person to provide, directly or indirectly, anything of value which shall accrue to the private advantage, benefit or economic gain of the official or any other person. This section does not apply to campaign contributions solicited or received consistent with federal, state or local laws.

5. PENALTIES FOR NONCOMPLIANCE—NO NEW LEGAL RIGHTS

a. In addition to any other penalty provided by law, violation of any provision of this document by any municipal official shall be a basis for disciplinary action including removal from his/her official position. Alleged violations will be addressed by an Ad Hoc Committee appointed by the Board of Selectmen on an as needed case-by-case basis. The committee will be composed of three persons, who are not affiliated with the circumstances. The committee findings shall be reported to the Board of Selectmen with recommendations as to what action should be taken.

b. Any official who violates this document may be subject to censure or removal from office as permitted by law.

6. CODE OF ETHICS SUPPLEMENTS EXISTING LAW

This document is intended as an addition to and supplements any federal, state, and local laws relating to the subject matter addressed herein. No provision in this Code of Ethics shall be construed to weaken or reduce other standards of official conduct, specific or implied, contained in any of the Municipal Ordinances/Policies

Chapter 7

Annual Reports

I have reviewed dozens of Municipal Annual Reports from many different communities and they are all different. 30-A MRSA §2801 requires that the officers of each municipality annually publish a complete report. Note the word "complete". There seems to be such a variance from community to community.

Annual reports should be considered as a "Historical Document". It provides a record of all that has transpired for a particular year and can serve as a great reference tool in the years ahead. I have enjoyed reading town reports from back in the 1800's and early 1900's. It is so interesting and exciting to learn what went on in many of these small communities over the last 100 years or more.

Although 30-A MRSA §2801 is vague when it says "complete", it does require that the annual report contain a record of all financial transactions of the community. Most communities provide a list of budgeted and actual expenses and revenues plus a list of employee salaries and vendor payments. I would also include a copy of the General Ledger Trial Balance for the end of the year and the status of any Special Funds and any Trust Funds. Most municipal computer software programs can provide this information. §2801 also requires a statement of Assets and Liabilities (These are usually contained in the Annual Audit Report).

It also requires a list of all delinquent taxpayers and the amount due from each. This means that the Tax Collector's report should include both the outstanding liens on real estate properties and the outstanding taxes on personal properties.

The Treasurer's report should include the outstanding liens from the previous years. §2801 also requires that the report contain any engineering and survey reports relating to the boundaries of the municipality and all related proceedings and actions of the Municipal Officers, together with any other information that the Municipal Officers consider to be of historical significance.

To accomplish this, the report should include reports from the Board of Selectmen/Town Council, Town Manager, other Municipal Officials, Chairperson of all Boards/Committees and any other organizations that receive funding from the community. Most annual town reports include annual letters from the local legislators. ss2801 requires that the annual report contain a statement that the complete post audit report from the last municipal year is on file in the municipal office. It also requires that the following excerpts from the audit report be included in the annual report:

a. Name and address of the auditor.
b. Auditor's comments and suggestions for improving the financial administration.
c. Comparative balance sheet.
d. Statement of departmental operations.

These should be considered minimal requirements. One interesting note in §2801, is that it prohibits printing the names of persons issued concealed firearms permits.

One of the things that is not mentioned in §2801 is the inclusion of any town meeting warrants. Historically, most towns that were and still are on a calendar year (Jan1-Dec31), included a copy of the upcoming years town meeting warrant, so that the citizens had a chance to review last years finances and actions to what was being proposed for them to vote on the upcoming year. By including the proposed warrant in the annual report, it saved the communities from having to print 2 separate documents. §2801 requires that copies of the annual report must be deposited in the municipal office or a convenient place of business for the distribution to the voters at least 3 days before the annual meeting. With most towns having their town meeting some time in March, it meant that they had to close out the financial accounts, get the audit completed, collect all the individual annual reports, get it all typed up and printed so that it would be available for distribution 3 days before the scheduled annual town meeting. By including the town meeting warrant for the upcoming town meeting in the annual report meant that the annual report would have to be available 7 days before the annual town meeting in order to meet the requirements of 30-A MRSA §2523, which requires that the town meeting warrant be posted 7 days prior to the town meeting. In the last 20 years or so, many towns have changed their fiscal year from (Jan1-Dec31) to (Jul1-Jun30) and have moved their annual town meetings to late May or early June. This has changed how many towns have included the town meeting warrants in their annual town report. Some towns still include copies of the current years town meeting warrant in their annual town report, some include both last years warrant and the current years warrant in their annual town report and some do not include any town meeting warrants. Even though there are no official requirements to include any town meeting warrants, I believe that from a historical point of view, the annual town report should include all town meeting warrants, including both special town meetings as well as the annual town meeting for that particular year, along with the "voting results".

Annual town reports can be a very important research tool. Copies are generally available at the local library or historical society as well as the municipal offices. Recently, I had the pleasure of delivering to the local historical society, over a hundred years of Town of Acton annual town reports, which came from a private collection.

The following is a suggested list of reports/information that is recommended for inclusion in the Municipal Annual Report, as a minimum:

- Dedication of the Annual Report
- Town/City Statistics
- Letters from Legislators/Members of Congress

- Letter from Board of Selectmen/Council
- Letter from Town Manager/Administrator/Mayor
- Directory—Contact Information
- List of Public Officials
- Assessor's Report (include Tax Commitment figures and Assessor's
- Notice for taxpayers to provide list of all taxable property)
- Town Clerk's Report
  - Vital Records
  - Marriage Licenses
  - Hunting/Fishing Licenses
  - Dog Licenses
  - Vehicle Registrations
  - Trailer Registrations
  - Boat Registrations
  - ATV Registrations
  - Snowmobile Registrations
- Registrar of Voters Report
- Tax Collector's Report
  - Tax Receipts
  - List of outstanding R.E. Property Tax Liens
  - List of outstanding Personal Property Taxes
  - List of Abatements
  - List of Supplemental Taxes
- Treasurer's Report
  - Revenue Report
  - Expense/Appropriation Report
  - General Ledger Trial Balance
  - Report of any Funds other than the General Fund
    - Cemetery Trust Funds
    - Scholarship Funds
    - Other
  - List of prior year's outstanding R.E. tax liens
  - List of town employee salaries
  - List of town vendors
- Code Officer's Report
- Health Officer's Report
- Town Forester's report
- Planning Department
- Board of Appeals
- Board of Assessment Review
- Fair Hearing Authority
- School Department
  - Superintendent's Report
  - Other
  - Financial Reports
    - Revenue Report

- Expense Report
- School Employee Salaries
- School Vendors
- Other
- Public Safety
  - Fire Department
  - Rescue Department
  - Police Department/Sheriff's Office
  - EMA Director
  - E911 Coordinator
  - Animal Control Officer
- Public Works
  - Public Works Director/Road Commissioner's Report
  - Solid Waste/ Transfer Station Manager
- Conservation Committee/Commission Report
- Recreation Committee Report
- Library Report
- Other Municipal Officials not listed
- Other Committees/Commissions not listed
- Non-Municipal Organizations that receive municipal funding
- Audit Report
- All Town Meeting Warrants pertaining to that particular year including voting results
- Town Meeting Warrant for current year, if the town is still on a Jan1-Dec31 FY

Chapter 8

Personnel Policy

Having a comprehensive personnel policy is a must and can prevent many of the personnel problems that might arise. After much research and review of other personnel policies, I developed the following comprehensive personnel policy for the Town of Acton. It may be modified to suit your circumstances.

Sample Policy

TOWN OF _____

PERSONNEL POLICY

Adopted: _____

Table of Contents

The Town of _____ specifically reserves the right to repeal, modify or amend these policies as necessary. These policies are intended as informational guidance and the Town reserves the right to interpret any provision and to change policies without prior notice or with reasonable notice when possible. These policies are not to be interpreted as promises of specific treatment or as creating any contractual rights with any employee/volunteer. In addition, conflicting changes in local, state or federal laws take precedence over the contents of personnel policies, whether or not those changes were incorporated into the policy.

Section I

Preamble and Purpose

1.1 Preamble

A. By action of the Town of _____ Board of Selectmen, the Personnel Policy (hereafter referred to as the "Policy") was voted into effect on _____. This Personnel Policy is established as guidelines to assist in developing sound working relationships between the municipality and its employees. These policies and subsequent modifications shall supersede any policy and/or rules made previously by the Board of Selectmen.

B. Elected officials and the Board of Selectmen in addition to all town committee members are not under the jurisdiction of the Personnel Policy. However, it is *expected* that these persons will utilize sound judgment in exercising their official duties and recognize relevant sections (e.g., Employee Conduct, Conflict of Interest, Harassment and Sexual Harassment, Confidentiality, Communications) of the Personnel Policy as a guide to the performance of their duty to serve the Town and its citizens. Standardized forms, definitions of terms and procedures, as well as certain legal mandates such as equal employment opportunity, worker's compensation, unemployment compensation, and safety requirements, are intended to apply to all employees unless inconsistent with a collective bargaining agreement.

Fire Department officers and Fire Department personnel along with Volunteer Rescue personnel, shall be subject to the Personnel Policy of the Town of _____. All other municipal volunteers, to the extent relevant and appropriate, are subject to this policy.

A copy of this policy shall be given to all town employees upon appointment.

Section II

Employment

2.1 Generally

A. Selection. The appointment of all personnel shall be the responsibility of the Board of Selectmen with input, as appropriate, from Department Heads/Municipal Officials. The Board of Selectmen may make appointments for one (1) year or may make it a regular full-time or part-time position without requiring an annual re-appointment.

The Fire Chief is appointed by the Board of Selectmen and shall be responsible for the recruitment, training, safety, discipline (under the direction of the Board of Selectmen) and the efficient functioning of the Fire Department, its members and personnel.

B. Application. All applicants must submit a written application for employment. Selection procedures will include a completed application, reference checks, submission of resume for supervisory positions. All applicants are encouraged to provide a resume, in addition to interview(s). The municipality relies upon the accuracy of information contained in the employment application, as well as the accuracy of other data presented throughout the hiring process and employment. Any willful misrepresentations, falsifications, or material omissions in any of this information or data may result in the municipality's exclusion of the individual from further consideration for employment or, if the person has been hired, termination of employment.

C. Tests. The municipality may where appropriate require applicants to submit to interviews, tests and examinations which may include, among others, written tests, agility tests, pre-employment but post-offer physical and/or psychological examination(s), and alcohol/drug testing as permitted under state and federal law when job related.

D. Probation period. All employees are considered probationary for the first six (6) months of employment. The probationary period shall be considered an extension of the selection process. Probationary employees may be removed at any time during the probationary period without cause and without right to file a grievance. Probationary employees are not eligible to take vacation or personal time. New probationary employees accrue vacation and sick leave but are not eligible to use vacation until after their trial period is completed. Sick leave accrual is subject to Section 8.3 of this Policy. Under extenuating circumstances, the probationary period may be extended with the approval of the Board of Selectmen, for no longer than 3 months.

E. Appointment of a new Town Clerk, Tax Collector or Treasurer. When appointing a new Town Clerk, Tax Collector or Treasurer, the Board of Selectmen will seek the advice and consent of the Warrant & Finance Committee.

2.2 Equal Opportunity Employer

The Town of _____ is committed to providing equal employment opportunities to applicants and employees. The town supports a policy of nondiscrimination in hiring, employment and personnel actions. The town is committed to the principal that each individual is entitled to equal employment opportunities without regard to: religion, race, sex, marital status, age, color, ancestry, national origin, creed, political affiliation, veteran status, sexual preference, or physical or mental disability.

This commitment applies to recruiting, hiring, compensation, fringe benefits, staff development and training, promotion, termination, and all other conditions of employment. This policy will be made known to all entities that do business with the Municipality.

2.3 Recruitment

The municipality shall employ the best-qualified persons who are available at the salary levels established for municipal employment. Taking time limitations into account, there shall be as wide a search for qualified candidates as is practicable. The character of the recruitment and selection process for all positions will vary contingent on the position, but may include advertising and open competitive examination in addition to contact with state and other employment offices and contact with special sources of information. In appropriate circumstances, the municipality reserves the right to hire from within, without externally posting the job vacancy. It shall be the duty of the Board of Selectmen (or Fire Chief under the direction of the Board of Selectmen) to seek out the most desirable employees/volunteers. Appendix (A) will be used as part of the selection process.

2.4 Employment Files

Employee files will be kept at the Town Hall in accordance to state and federal guidelines. A complete file will be kept in a secured area for each employee and will include items such as: verification of pay, hiring data, applications, resumes, reference letters, signed job descriptions, employee acknowledgement forms, probationary and annual review, letters of commendation and recognition, disciplinary actions, case notes and exit interview forms. Medical information, as well as Workman's Compensation information is part of the employee personnel file but, because of the confidential nature of such information, such material is kept in a secure location separated from the employee file.

All employees shall have job descriptions, that have been reviewed and approved by the Board of Selectmen.

An employee may, with reasonable notice to the Board of Selectmen and at a convenient time for the Board of Selectmen, review his/her employment file during regular working hours.

Employee files will be treated as confidential, to the extent permitted by law e.g. "Right to Know" mandates. Employee information is available only to the Selectmen and appropriate Department Heads/Municipal Officials.

Destruction of files for employees that have left the employ of the municipality shall occur according to state and federal guidelines.

2.5 Employment Classification

A. Probationary employees. All new employees and every person promoted or transferred to a new position are considered probationary for the first six (6) months of employment.

The probationary period shall be considered an extension of the selection process during which time employees will be subject to review and evaluation. In no case, will the probationary period be extended. If an employee's job is temporarily interrupted during the probationary period, upon return he/she will be required to complete the probationary period and may be given credit for the time already served. New probationary employees accrue vacation and sick leave but are not eligible to use vacation until after their trial period is completed. Sick leave accrual is subject to Section 8.3 of this Policy. Probationary employees may be removed at any time during the probationary period without cause and without right to a hearing.

B. Full-time. A full-time employee works a normal workweek of 35-hours a week and on a continuing basis. Such employees are subject to all personnel policies and rules and receive all benefits for which they satisfy required eligibility criteria.

C. Part-time. An employee in this classification works less than the normal 35-hour workweek, but on a continuing basis. Part-time employees are subject to all personnel policies and rules. A regular part-time employee working in excess of twenty (21) hours per week on a regular continuing basis receives benefits and rights as provided by this policy. This classification shall only be assigned at the discretion of the Board of Selectmen.

D. Temporary employees. Temporary employees, such as seasonal workers or "as needed" employees, work on a non-continuing basis, within a limited time frame usually not to exceed six (6) months. Temporary employees are subject to all personnel policies and rules but are not entitled to any benefits except those benefits required by law, including worker's compensation and unemployment compensation. Temporary employees may be terminated for any reason at any time.

E. Exempt employees. Are salary employees, who by the nature of their work, meet the "executive administrative or professional" exemption requirements of the federal Fair Labor Standards Act (FLSA). Such employees are deemed exempt from the payment of overtime for hours worked in excess of forty (40) hours in any week.

F. Non-exempt employees. All hourly wage earning employees who do not meet the "executive administrative or professional" criteria as set by the FLSA and, who are not otherwise exempt, or partially exempt from the overtime requirement of the FLSA, are eligible to receive overtime compensation paid at time and one-half (1.5) for hours worked in excess of forty (40) hours during any week. The Board of Selectmen **must preauthorize all overtime.**

G. Volunteers/Committee Board Members. Given the distinct nature of volunteer status, the municipality reserves the right to alter the procedures contained in this policy as is deemed necessary by the Board of Selectmen. The procedures contained herein shall serve only as a general guide to dealing with volunteers and may be altered on a case-by-case basis. Nonetheless, volunteers are expected to follow the rules of conduct contained in this policy.

2.6 Employee Evaluations

A. Generally. Evaluations will relate directly to the employee's position, work habits and job performance. Evaluations will be conducted by the employee's immediate supervisor with final review by the Board of Selectmen after a six-month probationary period for employees entering a new position, and annually thereafter. Once a written evaluation has been completed, the employee and person charged with performing the evaluation will meet to discuss the evaluation. After the reviewing agent has completed the reviews, the Board of Selectmen, individually, will have no more than 14 days total to review and return comments or sign, and if not done, the review stands. Evaluations will remain on file and be used as a tool to set performance goals. The employee's signature will be obtained which acknowledges review and understanding of the evaluation. Refusal of employee to sign will be noted.

B. Regular employees. All regular employees (full-time and part-time) will receive a written evaluation annually, on or about their anniversary date. Non-exempt employees shall receive their evaluation from the Department Head/Municipal Official. The Board of Selectmen will evaluate exempt employees. After the reviewing agent has completed the reviews, the Board of Selectmen, individually, will have no more than 14 days total to review and return comments or sign and if not done, the review stands.

C. Probationary employees. Newly hired probationary employees shall receive a 3-month review, although probationary employees may be terminated without cause and without advance notice. The 3-month review period should serve to guide a new employee so that he or she can attempt to correct any faults or shortcomings in their performance.

2.7 Whistleblower Protection

The Municipality strives to conduct its business with integrity and in strict compliance with all applicable federal, state and local laws and regulations. Accordingly, employees/volunteers are encouraged to bring to the attention of their Supervisor or the Board of Selectmen any actions of municipal officials or employees/volunteers that they believe may be improper or unsafe. The Municipality will not retaliate against any person who makes a report in good faith to either his Supervisor, the Board of Selectmen, or to a regulatory body.

2.8 Hiring of Relatives

The employment of relatives in the same department/office of an organization may cause serious conflicts and problems with favoritism and employee morale. In addition to claims of partiality in treatment at work, personal conflicts from outside the work environment may be carried into day-to-day working relationships. Therefore, the hiring of employees with a personal relationship with the supervisor within a department/office is strongly discouraged.

Relatives of persons currently employed by the Town of Acton may be hired for full time employment only if they will not be working directly for, supervising, or working in the same department as an immediate relative.

If the relative relationship is established after employment, The Board of Selectmen may transfer one of the affected employees if another position is available for which they are qualified.

In other cases where a conflict arises, even if there is no supervisory relationship involved, the parties may be separated by reassignment.

For the purposes of this policy, a relative is defined as spouse, children, stepchildren, parents, grandparents, grandchildren, brother, sister, brother-in-law, sister-in-law, aunt, uncle, nephew, niece, son-in-law, daughter-in-law, mother-in-law, father-in-law, step-parents, half-brother, half-sister, first cousin, or other persons residing in the same household. Relationships other than those defined shall be subject to the discretion of the Board of Selectmen.

Situations pertaining to this section which exist at the time of adoption of these policies shall be considered "grandfathered".

The Board of Selectmen, giving consideration to the recommendation of the appropriate Department Head/Municipal Official may make a finding that it is in the Town's best interest to hire the relative of an existing employee. Reason's, that the Board of Selectmen might make this finding, include but are not limited to the following:

☐ The relative has a skill or experience that is not attainable elsewhere.
☐ The relative is clearly the very best applicant for the position.
☐ The supervisory relationship is not direct or occurs infrequently.

This section does not limit or affect the authority or discretion of the Board of Selectmen.

Section III
Work Week & Attendance

3.1 Work Week.

The regular workweek for payroll purposes begins 12:01 am on Sunday and ends Saturday midnight. The actual hours for municipal employees shall be set by the Board of Selectmen. The normal office hours for the Selectmen, Town Clerk/Tax Collector and Treasurer are 9-4, T, W & F, Thursday evening from 6-8. The Selectmen's office and the Town Clerk/Tax collectors Office will also be open on the 1st and last Saturday of each month from 9-12.

3.2 Time Sheets.

For purposes of public accountability, all employees, exempt or non-exempt must record actual hours of work as well as paid or unpaid leave on their time sheets. Falsification of time records is a breach of Town policy and may result in disciplinary action including the possibility of dismissal. Time sheets are due no later than 10 am on the next Tuesday following the end of the workweek. Payday is, normally the next Friday following the end of the workweek. Any employee who fails to turn in timely time sheets may be subject to disciplinary action. All Time Sheets shall be signed by the Employee's Supervisor and reviewed by the Selectmen prior to the signing of the Weekly Warrant

3.3 Overtime.

A. Exempt employees: Exempt employees will not receive overtime pay, and are expected to work the number of hours required to perform the job. However, an exempt employee shall be entitled to one hour of compensation time for each hour worked in excess of their regular scheduled weekly hours. Compensation time may be accumulated up to eight (8) hours per calendar year. Compensation time will not carry over from one year to the other without approval by the Board of Selectmen. There shall be no payment for unused compensation time at the termination of employment for exempt employees.

B. Non-exempt employees: Employees not exempt from the Fair Labor Standards Act shall receive overtime pay at the rate of time and one-half (1 ½) in excess of thirty-five (35) hours per week. For the purpose of computing overtime, within any given week, only those hours spent on the job and actually worked will be used to calculate overtime pay. Vacation, sick leave, bereavement leave, holiday, military/jury leave and all other leave will not be counted toward calculating overtime pay.

C. Prior authorization. <u>Prior approval of the Board of Selectmen is necessary to authorize employee overtime and compensation time.</u> The Board of Selectmen will exercise discretion in authorizing overtime (and/or compensatory time if applicable). *Overtime shall be considered necessary only in critical situations where additional effort is needed to complete a task within a certain amount of time.* Temporary adjustments (i.e., same workweek) in working hours or realignment of duties within the department should be considered as alternatives to the use of overtime.

3.4 Attendance.

Employees shall be at their respective places of work at the appointed starting time and remaining at work until the end of the scheduled workday. It is the responsibility of employees who may be late or absent from work to see that their immediate Supervisor is advised of the reason for lateness or absence with as much advance notice as possible. If an absence, which has not been previously arranged for becomes necessary, within two (2) hours of the beginning of the employee's normal starting time or sooner if practicable, the employee is expected to contact their Supervisor. If an absence continues beyond one day, the employee is responsible for reporting in each day or providing the municipality with a physician's letter that contains the date the employee is to return to work. (Refer to the Medical Leave section for information on extended sick leave reporting requirements.) Repeated lateness, unexcused absences, absences without authorization or failure to return to duty within 24 hours may be cause for discipline and/or discharge.

3.5 Snow Days.

Employees may be excused from work due to snow days or severe weather at the discretion of the Board of Selectmen. Compensation for that absence will be considered as follows:

1. If the municipal building closes the doors to the public, effected non-exempt employees will not be compensated for the hours they normally would have worked.

2. When the municipal building is open, if an employee does not report for work, is offered the opportunity to leave work early and does so or is late arriving, non-exempt employees will not be paid for the absence. If possible, they may be offered the opportunity to make up the time or to utilize accrued paid time. Under the Fair Labor Standards Act, exempt employees are not subject to wage reduction due to inclement weather absences during a week where any regular work is performed. However, exempt employees are expected to demonstrate professionalism and good judgment with regard to the performance of their duties on such weeks.

3. Employees will be called when the municipal building is closed due to inclement weather.

4. The closing of the Transfer Station during snow days is left to the discretion of the Transfer Station manager.

3.6 Lunch & Break Periods.

Town Hall employees are entitled to a half (½) an hour paid lunch/meal period. One fifteen (15) minute break the first half of the work shift and one fifteen (15) minute break the second half of the work shift is permitted. Break time may not be taken at the beginning or end of a work shift, or immediately before or after a lunch break. Break time can not be accumulated to be applied toward an alternate work schedule. Break time is calculated as the time the employee is away from his/her workstation. Break time is not limited to only time spent at the place the break is taken.

Transfer Station employees are entitled to a half (1/2) an hour paid lunch/meal period.

3.7 Meetings, Seminars and Training Courses.

When the Town asks employees to attend these sessions for career development, payment will be for time spent at the course on the basis of a normal work day. Mileage will be paid at the rate set by the Board of Selectmen.

Section IV

Compensation

4.1 Payment Schedule.

The Town Treasurer, following the signing of the weekly expense warrant by the Selectmen, will issue payroll checks on Wednesday or Thursday. Paychecks will be released only to the employee whose name appears on the check unless other arrangements have been made by the employee in writing.

4.2 Payroll Adjustments.

Salary or hourly rate adjustments are appropriated by Town Meeting and the rate of adjustment is approved by the Selectmen. Adjustments shall be made at the beginning of each fiscal year by the Town Treasurer as directed by the Selectmen.

4.3 Deductions.

Employees may request deductions from their pay for payments to a credit union, property taxes, etc. These requests will be made to the Treasurer in writing.

4.4 Garnishment of Wages.

The municipality encourages all employees to manage their personal finances accordingly but will comply with all state and federal laws that apply to garnishment of employee wages.

4.5 Expense Reimbursement.

Employees shall be reimbursed for reasonable and authorized expenses incurred while carrying out official Town business. Reimbursement for use of a personal vehicle for Town business shall be at the per mile rate established by the Board of Selectmen, and expenses for tolls, parking, meals, lodging, etc. will be reimbursed at cost. Employees must submit receipts along with signed mileage sheet, approved by the Department Head and Board of Selectmen for reimbursement.

Section V

Employee/Volunteer Conduct

5.1 Generally.

Our taxpayers are entitled to the best service we can give them. Cooperation and teamwork by all employees/volunteers is essential to efficiency. Courtesy, responsibility, and unbiased treatment are the key elements of good service. All employees are expected and required to treat the public with promptness, patience, courtesy and respect. Employees are expected to conduct themselves at all times in a manner that will bring no discredit to their department or to the Town. Employees are prohibited from engaging in any conduct which could reflect unfavorably upon the Town or disrupt the efficient operation of the administration of the Town. Town employees must avoid any action which might result in or create the impression of using public employment for private gain, giving preferential treatment to any person or losing complete impartiality in conducting Town business.

5.2 Drugs & Alcohol.

It is the policy of the Town to recognize alcohol and drug abuse as a treatable disease. However, it is not the intent of the Town to accept below-standard performance nor to restrict supervisors in dealing with performance problems. Whenever appropriate, the Town shall refer employees to appropriate agencies and organizations to seek treatment. The use, possession, distribution, dispensing, sale, or working under the influence is strictly prohibited and is grounds for immediate dismissal.

The Town is committed to providing a drug-free, healthful and safe work environment. The term "drug(s)" also includes alcohol and prescription drugs when they are taken other than how they are prescribed. This policy applies during assigned work hours, on the Town premises and while conducting business-related activities off Town premises.

Employees/volunteers are required to report to work drug and alcohol free and free from the smell of alcohol. Job performance must be executed in a safe manner.

Employees seeking assistance for their substance abuse issues will be reasonably supported so that counseling appointments can be attended. Employees are accountable for their work performance whether they choose to participate in a substance abuse treatment program or not. Participation in a treatment program is voluntary and at the discretion of the employee.

The Town may discipline or terminate an employee/volunteer who is impaired or otherwise violates this policy or who exhibits an on-going performance issue.

Employees/volunteers using medication that may impair their work performance or pose a safety threat, should notify their Department Head. At the discretion of the Department Head with the approval of the Board of Selectmen, an employee/volunteer may be reassigned to a less hazardous task or be placed on sick leave if the impaired performance might pose a threat to oneself or others.

Employees who seek treatment may use their sick leave to attend a treatment program and may also be eligible for Family and Medical Leave Act (FMLA) or disability leave.

Employees are encouraged to discuss their questions or concerns regarding such leave with their Department Head.

Employees/volunteers must notify the Department Head or Board of Selectmen as soon as possible but no later than within five (5) days after any conviction for a drug/alcohol related offense.

5.3 Driving Policy.

Any employee, volunteer, official or other person who drives municipal vehicles, or drives private vehicles on municipal business, must have a valid Maine driver's license and a satisfactory driving record. Any person hired for a position, which involves driving municipal vehicles or driving a private vehicle for municipal business, shall have his or her license checked semi-annually for active status and accident/conviction history.

Any employee/volunteer cited or fined for a moving vehicle violation while on municipal time must report the event immediately to their Department Head. If any employee or volunteers' license is suspended or revoked while working for or providing services to the Municipality, such suspension/revocation must be reported within 24 hours to the Department Head. The Board of Selectmen shall determine the appropriate course of action, including reassignment of duties, leave of absence or discipline.

Any employee/volunteer driving a municipal vehicle, receiving mileage or other reimbursement from the Municipality for driving, or otherwise driving on behalf of the Municipality, shall wear seat belts at all times and shall require authorized passengers to wear seat belts. Unauthorized passengers such as family members, friends, etc. are not permitted without the authorization of the Department Head.

Any CDL licensed drivers are required to participate in a Town accepted drug testing program.

The Board of Selectmen may implement such other policies, as is necessary to ensure a safe driving policy.

5.4 Loss of License or Certification.

If it is a requirement for an employee/volunteer in a specific position to possess a valid license and/or class of license or certification, then it shall be a condition of employment for that employee/volunteer to maintain such license and/or certification. Failure to do so may result in re-assignment to an alternative position or job loss.

Employees who lose their license or fail to obtain re-certification as necessary, must immediately inform the Department Head of their new status.

5.5 Confidentiality.

Many municipal employees have access to confidential information pertaining to persons or property in the municipality. Employees/volunteers are prohibited from disclosing confidential information to *anyone* not having a need to know the information. The employees/volunteers must not use confidential or privileged information to their own private advantage or to provide family or acquaintances with private advantages. Employees/volunteers are charged with the responsibility of releasing, <u>upon approval of the Board of Selectmen</u>, only that information that is required under the "Right to Know" law (M.R.S.A., s/s 401-410).

5.6 Sexual Harassment

This Town is committed to promoting a workplace free from harassment. The Town of _____ recognizes the right of each employee, in addition to municipal volunteers, to work in an environment that is free from sexual harassment, including same sex harassment of employees, volunteers and or members of the public with whom the Town does business.

Harassment by Town employees/volunteers is prohibited and is considered unprofessional and unacceptable conduct. This policy specifically prohibits an employee or volunteer from engaging in any *intimidating, insulting, coercive* or *harassing behavior* that is sexual in nature. Remember, sexual harassment is in the 'eyes of the beholder' and not the way it may have been intended.

Examples of such prohibitive conduct include but are not limited to:

Any unwelcomed sexual advance or contact
Spoken or written comments about a person's sex
Showing or displaying pornographic or sexually explicit objects or illustrations in the workplace or while performing duties for the Town
Sexually offensive jokes, innuendoes, comments or visiting prohibited web sites
Sexually oriented comments about a person's body or behavior
Repeated requests for a date

Sexual harassment is a form of sex discrimination and is prohibited by Title VII of the Civil Rights Act of 1964 and Maine law. Sexual harassment includes any unwelcome sexual advances, requests for sexual favors, and other verbal or physical conduct of a sexual nature when:

Submission to such conduct is made either explicitly or implicitly a term or condition of an individual's employment or participation in other Town activities
Submission to or rejection of such conduct by an individual is used as the basis for employment decisions affecting such individual
Such conduct has the purpose or effect of unreasonably interfering with an individual's work performance or creates an intimidating, hostile, or offensive working environment; or
Such conduct violates any statute, regulation, ordinance, or any policy

Any employee or volunteer determined to have engaged in harassment of any kind and/or violence shall be subject to disciplinary action up to and including discharge. Department Heads are responsible for monitoring the behavior of their employees/volunteers. Inappropriate behaviors must be dealt with immediately.

The Town will work with you to resolve your complaint promptly and fairly.

This policy applies to the workplace during normal business hours, to all work related social functions whether on or off Town premises, and to business related travel.

5.7 Other Forms of Harassment.

Because the Town of Acton recognizes that each employee/volunteer has the right to work in a "safe" environment, any form of intimidation, hostility, unprofessional or obscene language will not be tolerated. Harassment related to race, color, sex, national origin, age, religion, ability/disability will not be tolerated. Violations of this policy will lead to disciplinary action including termination of employment and may also result in criminal prosecution.

Examples include but are not limited to:

> Harassment related to race, color, sex, national origin, age, religion, ability/disability
> Ridicule, slurs, offensive jokes, or derogatory actions
> Verbal threats, threatening behaviors, intimidation, acts of violence
> Refusal to work with or cooperate with another employee or volunteer on work assignments
> Inequitable disciplinary actions or work assignments

Violators of this policy may be removed from the premises and made to remain off Town premises until further notice pending the outcome of an investigation. Anyone who becomes aware of a potential threat must report it to his or her Department Head or to the Board of Selectmen.

Department Heads are responsible for monitoring the behavior of their employee/volunteers. Inappropriate behaviors must be dealt with immediately.

This policy applies to the workplace during normal business hours, to all work related social functions whether on or off Town premises, and to business related travel.

5.8 Workplace Violence.

Workplace violence is defined for the purpose of this policy as a literal act of violence against another individual(s) or against municipal property or a threat of violence against another individual(s) or against municipal property. This includes the use of physical force, harassment, intimidation or abuse of power or authority against another person. *Acts of violence in and around the workplace are unacceptable and will not be tolerated.* All such conduct will be thoroughly investigated and appropriate measures will be taken against employees/volunteers determined guilty of such offenses.

Suspected violators may be removed from the premises and may be made to remain off of Town premises until further notice pending the outcome of an investigation. Anyone who becomes aware of a potential threat must report it to his or her Department Head or to the Board of Selectmen.

Supervisors and Department Heads are responsible for monitoring the behavior of their employees. Inappropriate behaviors must be dealt with immediately. It is the responsibility of all employees, supervisory and otherwise, to foster a work environment of respect and healthy conflict resolution.

This policy applies to the workplace during normal business hours, to all work related social functions whether on or off Town premises, and to business related travel.

5.9 Complaint Procedures & Witness Obligations.

A. Complaints. If you believe you are being harassed, sexually or otherwise, we encourage you to complain promptly to your Supervisor, or to any member of management. You may also contact the Chairman of the Board of Selectmen at _____.

The Town is dedicated to working with you to resolve your complaint promptly and fairly. If you believe you are being sexually harassed, you also have the right to file a complaint with the Human Rights Commission (MHRC) within six months of the unlawful act or unlawful discrimination. To file a charge or obtain more information on the procedure, you may contact the Commission by mail at 51 State House Station, Augusta, ME 04333-0051, or by telephone at (207) 624-6050. You can also refer to the end of this policy for a copy of the MHRC procedures for filing a complaint.

If You Have Questions . . . Please feel free to contact the Board of Selectmen in person or by telephone at _____ if you have any further questions about what harassment/sexual harassment is, how our complaint process works, or about our policy against sexual harassment.

B. Witnessing Harassment. If a Town employee/volunteer witnesses what he or she believes to be harassment (sexual or otherwise) or witnesses workplace violence, the individual has an obligation to report this conduct to his or her Supervisor or to the Board of Selectmen. Supervisory and management staff aware of any form of harassment or workplace violence *must take immediate action to stop it.* Allegations will be promptly and discreetly investigated.

All employees or Town volunteers, who are asked, must cooperate in any such investigation and must maintain confidentiality regarding the investigation. All "good faith" reports can be made without fear of reprisal. Retaliation against witnesses or persons reporting such conduct in good faith is prohibited.

5.10 Workplace Safety & Injury Reporting.

A. Safety. Employees/volunteers will receive safety training including proper use of equipment, fire procedures, incident reporting procedures, and any other information necessary for employees/volunteers to adhere to a safe operating procedure. To use safety equipment as needed for their jobs, and to avoid willfully putting themselves or the municipality at risk of injury or liability, each employee/volunteer is expected to obey safety rules and to exercise caution in all work activities.

Employees/volunteers must immediately report any unsafe condition to his or her Department Head or the Board of Selectmen. Material Safety Data Sheets (MSDS) are on file in the Selectmen's Office.

Employees/volunteers who violate safety standards, who cause hazardous or dangerous situations, or who fail to report or, where appropriate, remedy such situations, may be subject to disciplinary action, up to and including termination. All "good faith" reports can be made without fear of reprisal.

B. Injury reporting. When an employee/volunteer of the municipality suffers an injury or accident in the course of employment, **regardless of how insignificant the injury may appear,** a report of the accident must be made immediately to the employee's/volunteer's Department Head or Board of Selectmen. Department Heads must, in turn, report the accident immediately to the Board of Selectmen so that any necessary accident and injury reports may be completed. Such reports are necessary to comply with laws and initiate insurance and Workers' Compensation benefits procedures.

5. 11 Ethics & Conflicts of Interest.

Municipal employees shall be covered by the requirements of 30-A M.R.S.A. § 2604 et seq. and the following: Representatives of the Town of Acton shall not knowingly participate in a conflict of interest situation without making a full disclosure to the Board of Selectmen. A conflict of interest is any situation whereby the representative of the municipality serves to benefit, or can be perceived as benefiting, from the situation that is in his/her control. Examples may include contracts, appointments, purchases and sales.

No Town employee or immediate family members of a Town employee on the Warrant and Finance Committee may vote on any department budget that the employee and/or family member may be involved with. Family members are defined under Section II; 2.8 Hiring of Relatives.

Any Board Member that may have a conflict of interest or appearance of conflict of interest shall provide full disclosure and should abstain from any further discussion or voting on the matter.

The Board of Selectmen have the right to take all steps necessary to ensure that a real or perceived conflict of interest situation is rectified.

5.12 Outside Employment & Solicitation.

A. Outside employment. No employee may engage in additional employment that in any way interferes with the proper and effective performance of the duties of his position, results in a conflict of interest or subjects the Municipality to public criticism or embarrassment. If the Board of Selectmen determines that such outside employment is disadvantageous to the Municipality, upon notification in writing by the Board of Directors, the employee involved shall take prompt steps to resolve the situation.

Any full-time or part-time employee who engages in employment outside of his regular working hours shall be subject to perform his or her regular municipal duties first. The Municipality shall not be liable for nor grant sick leave or disability leave in the case of any injury or occupational illness incurred by an employee/volunteer while engaged in outside employment.

B. Solicitation. No employee shall engage in any business other than regular duties of the Municipality during working hours, including such activities as selling to fellow employees/volunteers, lending of money for profit, etc. With the exception of municipally approved activities, no solicitation of any kind is permitted on municipal premises during working time. Working time includes the working time of both the employee/volunteer soliciting, and the employee/volunteer to whom such activity is directed. Working time does not include break time. While on municipal premises during non-working time, such as breaks and meal times, employees/volunteers may engage in personal, business or social activities that are not disruptive to those who are working.

5.13 Political Activity.

While performing their normal work duties, employees shall refrain from seeking or accepting nomination or election to any office in the Town government, and from using their influence publicly in any way for or against any candidate for elective office in the Town government. Town employees shall not circulate petitions or campaign literature for elective Town officials, or be in any way concerned with soliciting or receiving subscriptions, contributions, or political service for any person for any political purpose pertaining to the Town government. This rule is not to be construed to prevent Town employees from becoming, or continuing to be, members of any political organization, from attending political meetings, from expressing their views on political matters, or from voting with complete freedom in any election.

5.14 Gratuities/Gifts.

A town employee/volunteer is prohibited from soliciting or accepting any gift, gratuity, favor, entertainment, loan or any other item of monetary value from: any person who has or is seeking to obtain business with the town or, from any person within or outside town employment whose interests may be

> affected by the employee's/volunteer's performance or nonperformance of his official duties.
> Acceptance of nominal gifts in keeping with special occasions, such as marriage, retirement or illness or food and refreshments in the ordinary course of business meetings; or unsolicited advertising or promotional materials, e.g., pens, note pads, calendars, is permitted.

In addition, Supervisors must avoid placing themselves in a position that could interfere with, or create the impression of interfering with, the objective evaluation and direction of their subordinates. No Supervisor shall accept gifts from subordinates other than those of nominal value for special occasions, and no Supervisor shall borrow money or accept favors from any subordinate.

5.15 Smoking.

The municipality supports a smoke free work environment. Smoking is not permitted inside any town-owned building or any other structure under the control of the Town.

Town Hall employees wishing to smoke outside may smoke in a designated smoking area outside the Municipal Office Area specified by the Selectmen. There is no Smoking allowed on the grounds of the Transfer Station.

5.16 Municipal Property.

Employees and Town volunteers should not, directly or indirectly, use or allow the use of municipal property of any kind for other than official activities. Certain nominal use of municipal property may be permitted at the discretion of the Board of Selectmen so long as such use does not interfere with municipal operations. All Town property issued to the employee/volunteer such as keys, equipment, etc. shall be returned to the Town, in good repair, prior to the employee's/volunteer's last day. Failure to return Town property may result in private legal action against the employee/volunteer.

Employees/volunteers should not use the telephone facilities for personal calls when the placing of such calls would interfere with the employee's/volunteer's duties, would incur additional financial liability for the municipality or would interfere with the use of the facilities for official business. Any such use should be urgent, infrequent and of short duration.

5.17 Electronic Communications.

What is an "electronic communication"?
Telephones, pagers, communication radios, and voice-mail facilities;
E-mail;
Fax machines, modems, and servers;
City-supplied computers; and
Network tools such as browsers and Internet access facilities.

A. PURPOSE

Electronic mail, internet and telecommunication access are resources made available to Town employees to communicate with each other, other governmental entities, companies and individuals for the benefit of the Town.

B. POLICY

Email is designed to facilitate town business communication among employees and other business associates for messages or memoranda. Since no computer system is completely secure, the email system is not intended to transmit sensitive materials, such as personnel decisions or other similar information which may be more appropriately communicated by written memorandum or personal conversation.

The email system is Town property and intended for town business. The system is not to be used for employee personal gain or to support or advocate for non town-related business or purposes. **All data and other electronic messages within this system are the property of the Town of Acton.**

Email messages have been found to be public records and may be subject to the right-to-know laws, depending on their content.

In addition, the town, through its manager and department heads, reserves the right to review the contents of employees' email communications when necessary for town business purposes. Employees may not intentionally intercept, eavesdrop, record, read, alter or receive other person's email messages without proper authorization.

The Town of Acton purchases, owns and administers the necessary software and licenses to provide access to email and Internet services. Employees may not rent, copy or loan the software or its documentation. The town has invested time and money to secure its electronic systems form intrusion and harmful viruses. Therefore, employees may not provide alternative software to access the system. Employees may be held responsible for any damages caused by using unauthorized software or viruses they introduce into the town system. Department heads are responsible for the implementation and adherence of this policy within their departments.

C. PROCEDURES

1. General Information on Passwords: While you may have a confidential password, users should be aware that this does not mean that the system is for personal confidential communication, nor does it suggest that email is the property right of the employee. The use of the email system is for town business. Passwords should be periodically changed to ensure security of the email system. Users should not share their passwords with anyone other than as his or here department may require.

2. Internet: The Internet provides the town with significant access and dissemination of information to individuals outside of the town. The use of the Internet system for access and dissemination is intended to serve town business. Like all email messages, Internet messages are capable of being forwarded without the express permission of the original author. Internet messages are also routinely passed through routers before they reach their final destination. A message is "touched" many times before it gets to its recipient and the message author should be aware of this. Therefore, users must use caution in the transmission and dissemination of messages outside of the town and must comply with all state and federal laws.

3. Prohibited Uses: When sending email messages, appropriateness and good judgment should be used. Following are examples of Internet and email uses, which are prohibited:

> Communications that in any way may be construed by other as disruptive, offensive, abusive or threatening;
> Communications of sexually explicit images or messages;
> Communications that contain ethnic slurs, racial epithets or anything that may be construed as harassment or disparagement of others based on race, national origin, sex, age, disability or religious belies;
> Solicitation for commercial ventures, religious or political causes, outside organizations or other non job-related solicitations;
> Access to Internet resources, including web sites and news groups that are inappropriate in a business setting;

Any other use that may compromise the integrity of the town and its business in any way.

4. Retention of Email: Employees should be aware that when they have deleted a message from their workstation mailbox, it may not have been deleted from the central email system. The message may be stored on the computer's back-up system for an indefinite period. Note that email has been classified as "public documents, i.e. available to the media, in at least one state. Keep that in mind when you create or store email.

5. Web Site Development: The Internet is developing into an effective channel for the town to share information with citizens, visitors and customers. Departments are strongly encouraged to develop and keep up-to-date a departmental page as a link from the town's home page.

6. Applicability to employees, part-time employees, contractors and other users:
This email policy applies to all employees, contractors, part-time employees, volunteers and other individuals who are provided access to the town's email system. Third party should only be provided access to the email system as necessary for their business purpose with the town and only if they abide by all applicable rules.

7. Employee termination, leave of absence, vacation and other: Employees who leave employment with the town have no right to contents of their email messages and are not allowed access to the email system. The Board of Selectmen may access an employee's email if employees are on leave of absence, vacation, or are transferred from one department to another department and it is necessary for the town's business purposes.

8. Penalties: The misuse of the Internet or email privileges will be considered sufficient cause for discipline in accordance with the personnel policies and procedures and/or other applicable rules or laws. In addition, violation of this policy or misuse of the email system may be referred for criminal prosecution.

Section VI
Employee/Volunteer Discipline

6.1 Reasons for Disiplinary Action.

Disciplinary action usually begins with the Department Head who documents performance problems. Contemplated disciplinary action must be reviewed with the Board of Selectmen.

Disciplinary action up to and including dismissal may be initiated for reasons that include, but are not limited to the following:

- Absenteeism and/or tardiness
- Insubordination—The employee, without proper reason, refuses to perform a reasonable task or order when directed to do so by a supervisor.

- Unacceptable job performance
- Use of alcohol and/or non-prescriptive drugs during the work day or in any way which impairs the performance of the position
- Willful destruction of public and/or private property
- Falsification of documents, concerning the employee's application to the Town, payroll or other departmental operations
- Harassing and rude, obnoxious behavior including obscene language directed at employees, volunteers or members of the public
- Failure to comply with safety regulations and requirements
- Dishonesty of any kind or theft of Town, public or private property
- Acceptance of money or any gift by an employee/volunteer for any consideration afforded to the public, in general.
- Felony or misdemeanor conviction involving moral turpitude
- Employee is unable to maintain a cooperative attitude or working relationship with co-workers, supervisors, and the public.
- **Removal for the "Good of the Town". The Board of Selectmen with the authority to appoint,** prescribe the duties of, and when necessary for the good of the town, may remove any non-school officials and employees of the Town. Nothing in this personnel policy is intended or may be construed to limit the authority of the Board of Selectmen.
- Any other action or conduct materially affecting or impairing the efficiency of Town services or that brings the Town in public dispute or embarrassment
- Gossiping, either verbally or in written form is grounds for immediate dismissal.

6.2 Disciplinary Process

The disciplinary process may include, but is not limited to the following procedures:

A. Verbal Warning. The Department Head may verbally warn an employee/volunteer to improve specific performance issues or to rectify specific conduct. The date, time and nature of the warning shall be noted in the employee's personnel file. When possible, warnings should be given within two (2) days of the knowledge of the offense. The municipality reserves the right to move to a written warning, suspension or termination depending on the seriousness of the situation.

B. Written Reprimand. The Department Head may give a written reprimand to an employee/volunteer for a repeated offense, or for an offense serious enough to require more than a verbal warning. A reprimand will include the nature of the offense, date and time of the offense, possibility of future disciplinary action and steps for correction of the action. A copy of the reprimand signed by the Department Head and the employee/volunteer will be placed in the employee/volunteer personnel file. If the employee/volunteer refuses to sign the reprimand, this fact should be noted and witnessed on the reprimand. The municipality reserves the right to move to suspension or termination depending on the seriousness of the situation.

C. Suspension. The Board of Selectmen may suspend an employee/volunteer with or without pay for a recurring offense or an offense which merits suspension. Suspensions will be consistent with

FLSA requirements. The municipality reserves the right to move to termination depending on the seriousness of the situation.

The employee will have the opportunity to respond to the charges prior to serving the suspension unless the employee's actions are a threat to self or others. The employee's opportunity to respond to the charges may occur at a meeting with the employee held to discuss the reasons for the suspension. The length of suspension is based on the seriousness of the offense and what the Board of Selectmen may determine is warranted.

Employees will receive confirmation of their suspension period and the necessary corrective steps. Employees will be warned of the potential for more serious disciplinary action or dismissal in the event of further offenses. A copy of the letter of suspension will be included in the employee's personnel file. Suspension with or without pay may occur for an indefinite period pending complete investigation of the incident or offense.

D. Dismissal. The Board of Selectmen may dismiss an employee if his or her job performance or misconduct warrants dismissal. After a meeting between the employee, and Department Head, the employee shall be notified of the reason(s) for the dismissal and the effective date thereof. Dismissals shall be confirmed by the Board of Selectmen in writing prior to the effective date of dismissal.

All disciplinary action is normally taken in executive session of the Board of Selectmen unless the employee requests an open session.

E. Volunteers. Given the distinct nature of volunteer status, the municipality reserves the right to alter the procedures contained in this policy when dealing with volunteers. The procedures herein contained shall serve only as a general guide to dealing with volunteers and may be altered on a case-by-case basis.

Section VII

Employee/Volunteer Grievance Procedures

The Town recognizes that situations may arise in which an employee/volunteer believes that they have been treated unfairly in accordance to the Town's policies and procedures. The employee/volunteer should attempt to resolve the problem or complaint with their Department Head as appropriate. If the matter cannot be resolved, they may file a formal complaint.

7.1 Grievance and Complaint Procedure.

The purpose of the complaint procedure shall be to settle employee/volunteer complaints at the lowest practical level and as quickly as possible, promoting efficiency and good employee morale. The following procedures shall apply:

A. Complaints must be filed in writing with the Board of Selectmen, as soon as possible but, no later than five (5) working days after the incident or complaint has occurred.

B. The complaint of the aggrieved employee/volunteer must clearly state the specifics of the complaint. Once having received the complaint, the Board of Selectmen may find it necessary to meet with the employee/volunteer to discuss the matter. The Board of Selectmen shall render a written decision within thirty (30) calendar days when practical, or within a reasonable amount of time depending on circumstances.

7.2 Terminating Employment.

A. Generally. Employees may leave a job in a variety of ways including resignation, retirement, layoff, or discharge. When possible, a meeting with the Board of Selectmen will be conducted prior to the employee's last day. The purpose of the meeting(s) is to provide information regarding any benefits that are due to the employee, such as insurance coverage, and unused vacation. In addition, employees still in possession of municipal property are expected to return the property at this time. All Town property such as keys, equipment, etc. issued to the employee shall be returned to the Town in good condition prior to the employee's last day. Documentation of the meeting will be performed by the secretary to the Board of Selectmen and will become part of the employment file.

B. References. Reference requests should be submitted in writing to the Board of Selectmen. The Town will provide the following information on employment inquiries: Verification on dates of employment; job title and a description of duties. Further information will not be provided without a written release from the employee. No additional information will be furnished unless it falls within the guidelines of state and federal regulations governing public information about municipal employees.

C. Resignations/Retirement. Exempt staff are encouraged to provide at least one (1) month's notice of resignation. Non-exempt staff are encouraged to provide two (2) weeks of notice of resignation. Written notice should be provided to the Department Head who will then bring it to the attention of the Board of Selectmen. The Department Head will prepare a plan to ensure continuing coverage of the departmental work and will work with the Board of Selectmen to identify benefits owed the employee and to begin the recruitment process. All Town property such as keys, equipment, etc. issued to the employee shall be returned to the Town in good condition prior to the employee's last day.

D. Lay-Offs. Funding for some positions may change due to Town Meeting appropriations. Employees may face lay-offs due to many reasons including restructuring or budgetary reasons. The normal termination process outlined under Section 7.2 will be followed when possible.

E. Discharge. An employee may be discharged for a number of reasons, refer to Section VI.

Section VIII
Benefits

8.1 Vacation.

A. Generally. Vacation privileges are available to full-time employees and regular part-time employees working in excess of twenty (20) hours per week on a regular basis subject to the following conditions.

Eligible employees will earn paid vacation consistent with the following schedule:

One year of continuous service completed = 1 week of vacation time
Two years of continuous service completed = 2 weeks of vacation time
Five years of continuous services completed = 3 weeks of vacation time

B. Accrued Vacation Time. Vacation time shall accrue from the date of hire as a full-time employee or regular part-time employee working in excess of twenty (20) hours per week on a regular basis. Employees shall not receive vacation time until they have *completed their first year of employment* with the Town

Employees must take the vacation time due them within that year after the vacation time is earned. Vacation time may not be carried over to the next calendar year. Exception to this may be permitted for special circumstances with prior approval of the Board of Selectmen.

If an employee is absent from work, accrued sick time and/or vacation time/personal days must be used. Employees may be allowed to take unpaid leave, when approved by the Board of Selectmen, in cases where paid leave time has been exhausted. When an employee terminates employment with the Town of_____, they will receive whatever vacation pay they have accrued.

C. Scheduling. Vacations will be scheduled at such times to be mutually agreeable to the employees and their supervisors. Due consideration will be given to an employee's seniority in regard to scheduling vacations. Vacation leave will ordinarily be taken in blocks of one (1) or two (2) week periods, but vacations for a lesser period may be permitted by the Board of Selectmen for special reasons.

Employees must request vacation time from the Department Head at least two (2) weeks in advance to ensure appropriate staff coverage during the vacation period.

D. Vacation pay. Employees may receive their vacation pay prior to the start of their vacation, but must advise the Town Treasurer in writing, at least ten (10) days in advance.

E. Personal Days. Employees may use accrued vacation time as Personal Days.

8.2 Holidays.

Holiday pay is available to eligible exempt and non-exempt regular employees. Employees who do not work a full week will be paid holiday pay only if the holiday falls on the day the employee was scheduled to work. Compensation for holidays will be based upon the number of hours that the employee would have worked if the holiday occurred on a regular workday. Holidays within vacation time are not considered a vacation day. Eligible holidays are as follows:

A. Subject to these rules, the following holidays shall be paid holidays for regular Town employees. Note: The Board of Selectmen reserves the right to approve additional holidays.

New Years Day
Memorial Day
Independence Day
Labor Day
Veteran's Day
Thanksgiving Day
Christmas Day

A person on a leave of absence without pay shall not be entitled to holiday pay.

When occasion warrants, employees may be required to work whole or part of a holiday. Employees working a holiday shall receive pay at the time and a half rate, i.e., road commissioners, plow drivers, etc.

8.3 Sick Leave

A. Employee Eligibility. Paid sick leave for each regular full-time employee is earned at the rate of one (1) day for each calendar month of service in proportion to the hours worked and may accumulate to no more than 120 days. Part time employees will receive a prorated amount of sick days. Sick days are available in ½ day increments. This time cannot be used for vacation time. Sick days cannot be used the day before or the day after a holiday. Employees absent from work on the day before or after a holiday may be requested to provide a physician's note certifying that the reason for the absence was illness.

Sick leave is not an entitlement to be used at the discretion of the employee but may be granted by the Board of Selectmen for any of the following reasons: Personal illness or injury of a nature sufficient to justify absence from work; personal medical or dental appointments that cannot be scheduled other than during working hours.

After three (3) consecutive days of sick time, the Board of Selectmen may require a certificate from a qualified physician to justify continued absence and/or return to work. The municipality may request a physician(s) letter(s) certifying "fitness for duty" prior to an employee's return to duty after an extended or serious medical/psychiatric leave or where a "safety" issue presents itself.

B. Probationary Employees. New probationary employees shall not be entitled to paid sick leave until they have completed one hundred eighty (180) days of employment. At the completion of one hundred eighty (180) days employment, probationary employees' cumulative sick leave days shall be computed from the original date of employment. An employee must work twelve (12) or more full work days in that month in order to earn sick leave for that month.

C. Abuse of Sick Leave. Employees who are found to abuse or fraudulently use sick leave will be subject to disciplinary action up to and including termination.

D. Absentees. If an employee is absent from work, accrued sick time and/or vacation time must be used. Absences for a part of a day that are chargeable to sick leave shall be charged proportionately in an amount not smaller than one-half (1/2) day. Employees may be allowed to take unpaid leave, when approved by the Board of Selectmen, in cases where accrued paid leave time has been exhausted. Upon cessation of employment with the Town, employees will not receive accrued sick time pay.

8.4 Health Insurance

For all regular full-time employees or personnel defined as those employees averaging at least twenty-one (21) hours per week for fifty (50) weeks of the year, the Town will pay 100 percent (100%) of the single subscriber health insurance coverage and eighty-five percent (85%) of family subscriber coverage. The Board of Selectmen shall select the health insurance plan to be provided to employees.

8.5 Retirement

The Town does not contribute to a retirement fund for employees at the present time. Any employee that is 65 years of age and has 20 or more years of continuous service to the Town of _____may be entitled to retain their Health benefits at the Town's expense upon retiring.

8.6 Worker's Compensation

This program protects employees against income losses caused by job-related injuries and occupational disease. The Town's Workmen's Compensation carrier is Maine Municipal Worker's Compensation Fund. Report filing, processing, and review are governed by State guidelines. Employees are required to immediately report any incident or accident to the Department Head, or in the absence of a Department Head, to the Board of Selectmen regardless of how minor the injury. All injuries will be reported to Maine Employer's Mutual and the Selectmen within twenty-four (24) hours of the incident.

8.7 Unemployment Insurance

The Town provides unemployment compensation benefits to employees in accordance with state and federal law.

8.8 Social Security.

The Town participates jointly with employees in making Social Security payments. Participation in this program is mandatory.

8.9 Staff Development.

A. Job-related, Required Training: As a condition of employment, each employee shall attend and participate in training programs designated to be necessary for effective job performance by the Department Head or the Board of Selectmen.

B. Voluntary Training: The town will attempt to make opportunities available to the employees, within the constraints of the municipal budget, for further development of specific skills and expertise deemed of mutual benefit to the employee and the town. Approval for staff development involving expenditure of funds must be obtained from the Board of Selectmen.

C. Training and Development Expenses: All training and development expenses shall be approved in advance by the Board of Selectmen.

Section IX
LEAVES OF ABSENCE

9.1 Bereavement.

An employee may be excused from work for up to three (3) work days because of death in his/her immediate family, as outlined below, and shall be paid his/her regular rate of pay for the scheduled work hours missed. It is intended that this time off be used for the purpose of handling necessary arrangements and attendance at the funeral.

For purposes of this article only, immediate family is defined to mean spouse, parents, children, brothers, sisters, mother-in-law, father-in-law, grandparents, and grandchildren.

One work day may be granted to employees without pay at the sole discretion of the Board of Selectmen for attendance at funerals of persons not covered under the above definition.

9.2 Family & Medical Leave (FMLA)

As provided by the 1993 Family and Medical Leave Act (FMLA), all eligible employees shall be entitled to take up to 12 weeks of unpaid, job-protected leave during any 12 month period for specified family and medical reasons.

A. Covered Family and Medical Reasons. An eligible employee shall be entitled to 12 weeks of unpaid leave during a 12-month period for one or more of the following reasons:

1) The birth or placement of a child for adoption or foster care;
2) To care for an immediate family member (spouse, child, or parent) with a serious health condition;
3) To take medical leave when the employee is unable to work because of a serious health condition.
4) A serious health condition, which shall be defined as an illness of a serious and long-term nature resulting in recurring or lengthy absences. Treatment of such an illness would occur on an inpatient situation at a hospital, hospice, or residential medical care facility, or would consist of continuing care provided by a licensed health care provider.

An employee may take leave if a serious health condition makes the employee unable to perform the functions of his/her position. Employees with questions about whether specific illnesses are covered under this policy or under the Municipality's sick leave policy are encouraged to meet with the Board of Selectmen.

B. Employee Eligibility. An employee shall be entitled to family leave when he/she meets the following criteria:

The employee has worked for at least 12 consecutive months for the Municipality. If the employee was on the payroll for part of a week, the Municipality will count the entire week. The Municipality considers 52 weeks to be equal to twelve months.

When both spouses are employed by the Municipality, they are jointly entitled to a combined total of 12 work weeks of family leave for the birth or placement of a child for adoption or foster care, and to care for a parent who has a serious health condition.

C. Calculation of Leave. Eligible employees can use up to 12 weeks of leave during any 12-month period. The Municipality will use a rolling 12-month period measured backward from the date an employee uses any FMLA leave. Each time an employee uses leave, the Municipality computes the amount of leave the employee has taken under this policy, subtracts it from the 12 weeks, and the balance remaining is the amount the employee is entitled to take at that time. For example, if an employee has taken 5 weeks of leave in the past 12 months, he or she could take an additional 7 weeks under this policy.

D. Maintenance of Benefits. An employee shall be entitled to maintain group health insurance coverage on the same basis as if he/she had continued to work at the Municipality. To maintain uninterrupted coverage, the employee will have to continue to pay their share of insurance premium payments. This payment shall be made either in person or by mail to the Selectmen's office by the 15th (fifteenth) day of each month. If the employee's payment is more than 30 days overdue, the Municipality will drop the coverage.

If the employee informs the Municipality that he/she does not intend to return to work at the end of the leave period, the Municipality's obligation to provide health benefits ends. If the employee chooses not to return to work for reasons other than a continued serious health condition, the Municipality will require the employee to reimburse the Municipality the amount the Municipality contributed towards the employee's health insurance during the leave period.

If the employee contributes to a life insurance or disability plan, the Municipality will continue making payroll deductions while the employee is on paid leave. While the employee is on unpaid leave, the Municipality will request that the employee continue to make those payments, along with the health care payments. If the employee does not continue these payments, the Municipality will recover the payments at the end of the leave period, in a manner consistent with the law.

Certain types of benefits will not accrue during the leave period consistent with the Municipality's benefits policy. However, the use of family or medical leave will not be considered a break in service when vesting or eligibility to participate in benefit programs is being determined.

E. Job Restoration. An employee who utilizes family or medical leave under this policy will be restored the same job or a job with equivalent status, pay, benefits and other employment terms.

The Municipality may choose to exempt certain highly compensated, "key" employees from this job restoration requirement and not return them to the same or similar position at the completion of FMLA leave. Employees who may be exempted will be informed of this status when they request leave. If the Municipality deems it necessary to deny job restoration for a key employee on FMLA leave, the Municipality will inform the employee of its intention and will offer the employee the opportunity to return to work immediately.

F. Use of Paid and Unpaid Leave. If an employee has any accrued paid leave (e.g., sick leave, vacation) the employee will use paid leave first and take the remainder of the twelve weeks as unpaid leave.

G. Intermittent Leave and Reduced Work Schedules. In certain cases, intermittent use of the twelve weeks of family or medical leave or a part of a reduced workweek may be allowed by the Municipality. Employees wishing to use leave intermittently or to utilize a reduced work week for birth or adoption purposes will need to discuss and gain approval for such use from the employee's Department Head and the Board of Selectmen.

Employees may also use family or medical leave intermittently or as part of a reduced workweek whenever it is medically necessary. If the need to use leave is foreseeable and based on preplanned and prescheduled medical treatment, then the employee is responsible to schedule the treatment in a manner that does not unduly disrupt the Municipality's operations.

In some cases, the Municipality may temporarily transfer an employee using intermittent or a reduced workweek to a different job with equivalent pay and benefits if another position would better accommodate the intermittent or reduced schedule.

PROCEDURES:

H. Procedure for requesting leave. All employees requesting leave under this policy must complete the Family/Medical leave form available from the Board of Selectmen.

When an employee plans to take leave under this policy, the employee must give the Municipality thirty (30) days notice. If it is not possible to give thirty (30) days notice, the employee must give as much notice as is possible. An employee undergoing planned medical treatment is required to make a reasonable effort to schedule the treatment to minimize disruptions to the Municipality's operations.

While on leave, employees will be requested to report periodically to the Municipality regarding the status of the medical condition, and their intent to return to work.

I. Procedure for Notice and Certification of Serious Health Condition. On occasion, the Municipality may require the employee to provide notice of the need to utilize leave (where it is possible to know beforehand) and/or may require the employee to provide certification of an employee's serious health condition by a qualified healthcare provider. The employee should try to respond to such a request within seven (7) days of the request, or provide a reasonable explanation for the delay.

Qualified health care providers include: doctors of medicine or osteopathy, podiatrists, dentists, clinical psychologists, optometrists, and chiropractors, nurse practitioners and nurse-midwives authorized to practice under State law and performing within the scope of their practice under state law.

When seeking certification of a serious medical condition, an employee should ensure that the certification form contains the following:

1) Date when the condition began; expected duration; diagnosis; and a brief statement of treatment.
2) The certification should include a statement that the employee is unable to perform the essential functions of the employee's position and why.
3) If taking intermittent leave or working a reduced schedule, certification should include dates and duration of treatment and a statement of medical necessity for taking intermittent leave or working a reduced schedule.

If deemed necessary, the Municipality may ask for a second opinion. The Municipality will pay for the employee to get a certification from a second doctor, which the Municipality will select. If there is a conflict between the original certification and the second opinion, the Municipality may require the opinion of a third doctor. The Municipality and the employee will jointly select the third doctor, and the Municipality will pay for the opinion. The third opinion will be considered final.

9.3 Leave Without Pay.

If an employee is absent from work, accrued sick time and/or vacation time must be used. Employees may be allowed to take unpaid leave, when approved by the Board of Selectmen, in cases where paid leave time has been exhausted.

At the discretion of the Board of Selectmen, a full-time or part-time employee may be granted a leave of absence without pay, not to exceed sixty (60) days. The employee is expected to return to work at the end of this period. Continued absence without having arranged for an extension of leave may be deemed a resignation from the service. Employees may choose to continue insurance benefits during this leave by paying the full premium. Vacation and sick leave will not continue to accrue during the leave.

9.4 Jury Duty.

Regular employees chosen for jury duty will be released from their job duties for the time period of service, as determined by the court. The leave is not a benefit and the employee is expected to return to work immediately following release from jury duty. The Town will pay the difference between the employee's daily pay and the amount of daily pay for jury duty. The employee must present to their Department Head or to the Board of Selectmen an official statement of the jury pay received.

9.5 Military Leave.

The Uniformed Services Employment and Reemployment Rights At of 1994 (USERRA) grants rights to civilian employees whose employment is interrupted for military service or training. USERRA applies to all types of "service in the uniformed services" defined as the performance of duty on a voluntary or involuntary basis in any of the uniformed services.

Employees are entitled to a leave of absence for up to five (5) years with each employer for authorized service and military training in the uniformed services. More than five (5) years may be required if necessary to complete a period of obligated service.

Under USERRA a person leaving a civilian job in order to enter military serve or training is entitled to return to his civilian job after discharge or release from active duty if the following criteria are met:

Employees returning from military leave of absence are generally entitled to immediate or prompt reinstatement as long as:

Advance notice was given of the need for the leave

Cumulative service in the uniformed services is not more than five (5) years with the same employer (excluding certain active duty, training and other types of obligated service)

He/She either returns to work or reapplies for employment within the time prescribed by USERRA

He/She did not receive a dishonorable discharge

The pre-service position was other than temporary

A part-time or full-time employee who is a member of the military reserves or in the National Guard, and who is required to undergo field training during normal work hours, shall be entitled to a leave of absence with differential pay for the period of such training.

Differential pay is not to exceed two (2) weeks in any one (1) year. The Town will pay the difference between compensation for military activities as shown by a statement issued by military authorities giving his/her rank, pay and allowances and the amount of net straight time pay due as an employee of the Town. If the compensation for military service is equal to or greater than the net straight time salary or wages due as a town employee, then no payment will be made. Employees are entitled to unpaid leaves of absence to perform military duties to the extent required by law.

It is expected that the employee will return to work at the expiration of the approved leave. Should the employee be unable to return to work at the expiration of the Leave, it will be the employee's responsibility to request an extension from the Department Head or the Board of Selectmen.

9.6 Victims of Family Violence.

The Town recognizes that an employee may find it necessary to protect themselves or an immediate family member from domestic violence. In doing so, all reasonable efforts shall be made by the employee to preserve employment and the Town will comply with the laws and by making a reasonable effort to work with an employee during the immediate crisis. Employees will be granted reasonable and necessary leave from work with pay to:

a) Prepare for or attend court proceedings
b) Receive medical treatment or to attend medical treatment for a victim if it is the employee's daughter, son, parent, spouse or in the same household
c) To obtain necessary services resulting from domestic violence, sexual assault, stalking, or any act that would warrant an order of protection.

Unless to do so would:

a) Result in the Town sustaining undue hardship from the employee's absence
b) The request for leave is not communicated to the Department Head within a reasonable time under the circumstances
c) The requested leave is impractical, unreasonable or unnecessary based on the facts that are made known to the Board of Selectmen.

The Department Head or the Board of Selectmen must be notified of possible risks of violence, intimidation, harassment, etc. by the perpetrator of family violence so that measures may be taken to protect the victimized employee, staff, customers and property.

9.7 Emergency Disaster Volunteer Leave.

Under Maine law (30-A M.R.S.A. § 2705) a municipal employee who is a certified disaster service volunteer of the American Red Cross, upon the request of the American Red Cross in order to participate in specialized disaster relief services for the American Red Cross may, with the approval of the legislative body of the municipality or municipal officers:

Be granted leave not to exceed 15 days in each year without loss of pay, vacation time, sick leave or earned overtime accumulation;

Be granted a leave using that employee's compensated time off, with the employee's consent;

Be granted a leave using a combination of paid leave and compensated time off.

It is important to note that the relief services contemplated by this statute must be related to a disaster declared by the governor of a state or territory or by the President of the United States.

9.8 Emergency Disasters

The Board of Selectmen, with the advice and consent of the Warrant and Finance Committee, shall reimburse members of the _____ Fire and Rescue for any National Disaster or State of Emergency, or other fire emergency that exceeds (8) eight hours in duration, at the same rates established for the highway department. Firefighters or rescue members to be paid at the same rate as laborer; apparatus operator to be paid at the same rate as equipment operator; officers to be paid at the same rate as Road Commissioners. Funds to come from Undesignated Fund Balance (unappropriated surplus).

Section X
EMPLOYEE INPUT-SUGGESTIONS

It is the intent of this policy to cover most aspects of employment, but employee input in the form of constructive suggestions regarding working conditions or these personnel policies is both encouraged and welcomed. Comments and/or suggestions should be forwarded in writing to the Board of Selectmen.

Adopted on:

_____

_____

_____

Chapter 9

<u>Job Descriptions</u>

It is essential that all employees have a job description. It is an important responsibility for an effective manager to ensure that all employees have an up to date job description that clearly delineates their duties and responsibilities. MMA has several job descriptions from different communities that may be used as a guide in developing one for your organization. I also have copies of job descriptions for most municipal positions, which I am willing to share. I am also available to assist in the development of any job descriptions that you may need help with. I may be contacted at (207) 636-3205 or ran@ metrocast.net.